ADOLPHE ADAM
AND LÉO DELIBES

GARLAND COMPOSER
RESOURCE MANUALS
(Vol. 5)

GARLAND REFERENCE LIBRARY
OF THE HUMANITIES
(Vol. 681)

GARLAND COMPOSER RESOURCE MANUALS

General Editor: Guy A. Marco

1. *Heinrich Schutz: A Guide to Research*
   by Allen B. Skei

2. *Josquin Des Prez: A Guide to Research*
   by Sydney Robinson Charles

3. *Sergei Vasil'evich Rachmaninoff: A Guide to Research*
   by Robert Palmieri

4. *Manuel de Falla: A Bibliography and Research Guide*
   by Gilbert Chase and Andrew Budwig

5. *Adolphe Adam and Léo Delibes: A Guide to Research*
   by William E. Studwell

ADOLPHE ADAM
AND LÉO DELIBES
A Guide to Research

William E. Studwell

GARLAND PUBLISHING, INC. • NEW YORK & LONDON
1987

Library of Congress Cataloging-in-Publication Data

Studwell, William E. (William Emmett), 1936–
  Adolphe Adam and Léo Delibes.

  (Garland composer resource manuals ; v. 5) (Garland
reference library of the humanities ; v. 681)
  Includes index.
  1. Adam, Adolphe, 1803–1856—Bibliography.
  2. Delibes, Léo, 1836–1891—Bibliography. I. Title.
II. Series. III. Series: Garland reference library of
the humanities ; v. 681.
ML134.A34S8 1987   016.7821'092'2   86-9917
ISBN 0-8240-9011-X (alk. paper)

Printed on acid-free, 250-year-life paper
Manufactured in the United States of America

CONTENTS

Contents

ACKNOWLEDGMENTS

The author wishes to express his appreciation to the
several persons and organizations who were of assistance in
the production of this book. Dorothy Jones, Joan Williams,
and Violet Lange of the Music Library, Northern Illinois
University, and Myrtie Podschwit and her staff of the Inter-
library Loan Department, Northern Illinois University,
rendered various valuable services. Iris Saunders of DeKalb,
Illinois very competently prepared the manuscript. Dr. Guy
Marco's sage comments on the manuscript were extremely
helpful. And David A. Hamilton of Northern Illinois
University kindly gave advice on the indexes. Among the
organizations providing materials or information were the
state university system of Illinois, Northwestern University, the New York Public Library, and the Bibliothèque
nationale, Paris.

PREFACE

The genesis of this book occurred a quarter of a
century ago. The hearing of the prelude to **Sylvia** on a New
York classical radio station several times during 1961
caused this author to investigate the background of the
composer, Léo Delibes. Upon discovering that there was
relatively little literature on Delibes, this author pro-
gressively researched the 19th century master with the
ultimate goal of at least partially rectifying the scarcity.
The study of Delibes naturally led to a similar appreciation
of his friend and mentor, Adolphe Adam.

The twenty-five year odyssey is completed with this
publication on Adam and Delibes. As far as is known, this
is the first reference book in any language on either composer and the first substantial general English-language
work on either except for a recent American thesis on
Delibes.

Each composer has a separate section consisting of: an
overview (four essays); an annotated and complete listing of
musical works (including unrelated derived works); a selective, annotated and tightly organized bibliography (402
citations for Adam, 352 for Delibes); and general information (research lacunae, library resources for research,
personal name dictionary, and notable performances).

The key portions of both sections are the bibliographies, which include a wide variety of material: old and
new works; rare and common items; primary and secondary
sources; basic and specialized information; books, parts of
books, articles, scenarios/librettos, and scores of music
adapted from Adam's or Delibes' music. Excluded were:
scores and recordings of their music, which can be easily
accessed under the composers' names; visual materials like
films and illustrations unless they were part of or the
subject of a book or article; other non-print material and
ephemera. If an item in the bibliographies could not be
obtained, an annotation was supplied based on the best data
available. Author, title, and subject indexes for both
bibliographies are at the end of the book.

The criteria for inclusion in the bibliographies

depended on the type of material and the topic involved. At
least one edition of all books completely or substantially
on the composers and/or their works was included, with
juvenile books not being bypassed. A good sampling of
scenarios/librettos was also included. For parts of books,
articles, and other sources, the criteria were based on
three factors. One, primary and contemporary materials,
because of their special value, were comprehensively
inserted, while secondary and more recent items were
regarded in a far more selective light. Two, the sections
of the bibliographies with more extensive literature
(general works, **Giselle, Coppélia, Sylvia, Lakmé**, etc.) were
treated much more selectively than the sections with less
literature, which were treated comprehensively or semi-
comprehensively. Three, some special topics such as
derivatives and adaptations, substantial musical analysis,
and choreography tended to be comprehensively included
because they are often hard to find. The overall purpose of
the bibliographies is to provide as well as possible a
balanced and complete selection of sources which will be
useful to both the casual data seeker and the serious
researcher.

ADOLPHE ADAM

ADOLPHE ADAM

*Lithograph from a drawing by Cauvin, based on a contemporary
photograph of the composer*

OVERVIEW

ADAM'S LIFE AND WORKS IN SUMMARY

Although born to a musical family in Paris, one of the world's music centers, Adolphe Charles Adam (July 24, 1803–May 3, 1856) did not find the path to a musical career an automatic one. His father, Jean Louis Adam, a distinguished pianist and teacher (and also a composer of some accomplishment), strongly tried to keep his son from entering the musical profession. Ultimately, Adolphe received his father's permission to study music seriously, with the proviso that Adolphe remain an amateur and not compose for the theater. At seventeen, he entered the Paris Conservatory, where his chief teacher was François Boieldieu. Before he was twenty-one, he began composing music for the Paris vaudeville theaters, thus ignoring the promise made to his father only a few years before.

From January 22, 1824, to February 6, 1829, he contributed to twenty-three light musical productions for these theaters. His first work of consequence was the opéra comique **Pierre et Catherine**, produced at the more prestigious Opéra-Comique theater on February 9, 1829. From then on until his death, most of his theatrical works were produced at the Opéra-Comique and the even more prestigious Opéra, a clear sign that he had reached the higher levels of his genre. The only major exceptions to this pattern were a period of political instability in the early 1830s, a trip to Russia and Germany in 1839–1840, and a period of several years after 1844 when a dispute with the director of the Opéra-Comique led Adam to open his own theater, which failed. His first highly successful work was **Le chalet**, an opéra comique produced on September 25, 1834. Two years later, he wrote his most renowned operatic work, the opéra comique **Le postillon de Lonjumeau**, which premiered on October 13, 1836. Subsequent operatic works of note were the opéras comiques **Giralda** (July 20, 1850), **La poupée de Nuremberg** (February 21, 1852) and **Si j'étais roi** (September 4, 1852). His few attempts at serious opera gained little attention. Overall, he was an "eminent composer of comic operas"[1] who dominated the Parisian musical scene for at least a generation. In the long run **Le chalet** was to be Adam's most successful operatic work in

5

France, **Le postillon** the most successful throughout the
world and the most highly regarded, and the overture to **Si
j'étais roi** the most popular orchestral piece.

Adam's greatest fame, however, came in the area of
ballet. His best known work, and the best musically, is his
ballet **Giselle**, which was first produced at the Opéra on
June 28, 1841. This innovative and original masterpiece of
the romantic period, with a score of intrinsic artistic mer-
it, is the oldest consistently performed ballet today, and
is regarded as one of the very finest ballets of all time,
one of the true classics of the choreographic repertory.
Some of his other ballets also were skillfully composed and
were well received, notably **La jolie fille de Gand** (June 22,
1842), **Le diable à quatre** (August 11, 1845), **La fileulle
des fées** (October 8, 1849) and most of all **Le corsaire**
(January 23, 1856).

In total Adam, who was a facile composer and a hard
worker, produced 71 operatic works, 15 ballets, 6 cantatas,
11 pieces of religious music (including the very famous 1847
carol **Cantique de Noël**),[2] at least 65 songs/minor vocal
pieces, about 200 light piano works, at least 7 works for
harmonium, 9 rearrangements/reorchestrations of the
theatrical works of others, 5 secular choral works, plus a
few other works, all in a time span of thirty-two years. Of
these, only several operas, several ballets and **Cantique
de Noël** are given much attention in the late twentieth
century.[3]

ADAM'S RELATIONSHIPS TO HIS CONTEMPORARIES

During his eminent musical career, mostly associated
with the theater, he came in contact with many persons.
Much of what he felt and observed in the course of these
contacts was preserved for posterity in his various well-
crafted writings, which include his commentary on his
contemporaries.[4] Of all his associations, his two most
important artistic relationships were with his teacher
François Adrien Boieldieu (1775-1834) and his pupil Léo
Delibes (1836-1891).

Boieldieu, a prominent composer of light operatic
works, was more than Adam's instructor in composition and
chief teacher at the Paris Conservatory. He was also one of
Adam's closest friends, though twenty-eight years older.[5]
Most significantly, Boieldieu was the principal influence on

Adam's development as an operatic composer. In 1825 the
master gave the pupil some very practical experience by
allowing him to work on the highly successful opera
La dame blanche. By a benevolence of fate, Boieldieu,
though ill for years, lived just long enough to witness
Adam's first outstanding work, **Le chalet.** Boieldieu was
thus assured that he had successfully transferred his legacy
in light opera to his younger cohort.

     Delibes' relationship to Adam was similar to Adam's
association with Boieldieu. Soon after Delibes' father died
in 1847, Delibes' family moved to Paris and young Léo
attended the Conservatory in 1848. After a while, Delibes
studied composition under Adam, and Adam became his mentor
and probably also a substitute father. Through Adam's contacts, Delibes obtained two professional positions in 1853,
one as organist at the Church of St. Pierre de Chaillot and
another as accompanist at the Théâtre-Lyrique. And when
Delibes was approached to compose the music for a minor
theatrical work, he consulted his master Adam as to whether
he should accept the offer. Adam, of course, advised him to
go ahead and the resultant work, **Deux sous de charbon,** was
first presented on February 9, 1856. In a strikingly
similar parallel to that of Boieldieu and Adam, Adam died
less than three months after Delibes had been initiated into
his career as a composer. Adam's legacy to Delibes was the
musical theater, but not just the genre of opera. The
greater influence of mentor on pupil in this case was in
ballet. Prior to Delibes, who eventually became the father
of modern ballet music, Adam was the most accomplished
composer of ballets. Surely something of Adam's skill in
and propensity for ballet music, particularly the musical
excellence and advances in **Giselle,** must have been passed on
to his prize pupil.[6]

ADAM'S MUSIC

     When the whole spectrum of commentary on Adam's music
is viewed, it is hard to believe that only one person is
involved. Excluding his main biographer, Arthur Pougin, who
expectedly has a high regard for Adam's music,[7] the gamut of
opinion, running from negative to positive, is as follows:

          Edwin Evans (1939): Concerning **Giselle,** he says that
          "the survival of the ballet is due to the dancers,
          not the music"; also, that with a few exceptions,
          "oblivion has overtaken the composer."[8]

Henri De Curzon (1933): Adam's music is "essentially superficial"; also, "one sees there too
constantly that this excellent musician was never
an artist."[9]

François Joseph Fétis (1873): Describes Adam's
music as "jolies melodies" (happy tunes) and
"gracieuses bagatelles" (gracious trifles).[10]

Humphrey Searle (1958): "There is no doubt that
the continued success of **Giselle** depends far more
on its dancing than on its music"; yet he immediately follows with, "Nevertheless, Adam's score for
Giselle is, at least, extremely competent."[11]

Roger Fiske (1958): On **Giselle**, he states that
"the music, though far from great, is wonderfully
effective in its place, and decidedly better than
most ballet music of its day.[12]

David Ewen (1966): Has a sufficiently high opinion
to include him in a reference work on "great composers," yet feels that "what he lacked most were
dramatic power, emotional depth, and genuine
creative originality."[13]

David Ewen (1961): Describes Adam as "a master
of expressive and dramatized melodies."[14]

Walter Terry (1968): Concerning **Giselle**, he states
that "its sounds are marvelous guides to the steps,
gestures, moods, and dramatic surges of one of the
greatest dramatic ballets of all time."[15]

This array of commentary, sometimes self-contradictory,
is further muddled by the changes of opinion of persons and
publications after a period of time has elapsed. Serge
Lifar, in his 1942 book **Giselle: Apothéose du ballet romantique**, has a very unfavorable opinion of Adam's music.[16]
Yet in his 1955 book, **La musique par la danse**, his view of
Adam is considerably more moderate.[17] Even more pronounced
is the metamorphosis in Grove's **Dictionary of Music.** The
first edition (1890) stated that "his melodies are frequently trivial to absolute vulgarity."[18] In the fifth
edition (1954) an essay by Francis Hueffer is overall much
more appreciative of Adam, though at the same time claiming
Adam's artistic style was "frequently fatal to his higher
aspirations."[19] And in the **New Grove Dictionary** (1980) the

opinion has completed its 180 degree turnaround to Elizabeth
Forbes' laudatory comments on Adam's music: "graceful and
charming"; "eminently danceable music"; and that several of
Adam's operas and ballets have "scores full of genuine
inspiration."[20]

A trend is clearly evident in the body of opinion
given above.   Generally, earlier attitudes are less favorable than more recent ones.   To some extent this goes along
with the resurgence of interest in nineteenth century ballet
which has been evident lately.   Also, like many cultural
phenomena, the opinion about Adam over the past 150 years
has been subject to the complete intellectual cycle from
high praise to excessive criticism to a more balanced and
fair attitude.   Note that composers like Tchaikovsky and
Mahler are more highly regarded now than several decades
ago, although for different reasons.

Clearly at least some of Adam's music is good enough
to have survived well over a century of changing tastes.
Despite protestations to the contrary, Adam's works are to a
fair extent still with us.   **Cantique de Noël,** one of the
finest carols, remains highly popular.   **Le postillon de
Lonjumeau,**[21] **Si j'étais roi,**[22] and even **La poupée de
Nuremberg**[23] have been at least occasionally produced in
the post–World War II period.   This is significant, for
light operatic works tend to fade away after a while.   For
example, the works of Victor Herbert, Rudolph Friml, and
Sigmund Romberg were very popular in the first half of the
twentieth century, but now are seldom performed.

The excellence (or at least the endurance) of **Giselle**
cannot be refuted, and it is a three-sided excellence --
plot, dancing, and music.   In addition, the other ballets
have not been completely forgotten.   Since 1945, **La jolie
fille de Gand,**[24] **Le diable à quatre,**[25] and **Le corsaire**[26]
have been performed at least in excerpts.   Furthermore, the
music of the ballets other than **Giselle** is worthwhile, as
explained by Elizabeth Forbes: **"La jolie fille de Gand, La
filleule des fées,** and **Le corsaire** have scores, if not
plots, of similar quality to those of **Giselle."**[27]   To this
list, possibly, could be added at least some parts of **Le
diable à quatre.**

A final bit of analysis may be appropriate.   The most
serious and recurring criticism of Adam's work is his al-
leged lack of dramatic power and depth.   To some degree this
criticism is unfounded.   Adam is certainly not devoid of

such characteristics, as is evident in **Giselle, Le corsaire**
and **Cantique de Noël,** among others. At the same time it
cannot be reasonably claimed that depth abounds in his
music. Humphrey Searle probably best describes the dilemma
of Adam's reputation for shallowness when he observes, in
reference to **Giselle,** that "the simplicity of the music here
does disguise a greater dramatic power than many people
realize."[28] Searle's analysis helps to clarify the situation and gives more respectability to Adam's music, yet it
is difficult to deny that the criticisms are partially
valid. Much of the explanation for the lesser depth, in
addition to the overall lighter nature of his works, could
be his orchestration/instrumentation. Generally, his
orchestrations are less full, less complex, and less rich
than they should be. (It is indeed ironic that one of his
major weaknesses was one of the major strengths of his
protégé, Delibes). If he had given more attention to this
facet of his music, quite possibly his works would have
become more deep and dramatic. Perhaps Noël Goodwin was
touching on this point when he commented that the music of
Giselle "may not be the most rewarding of ballet music for
the orchestral player, but it does belong to that category
of music...that the better it is played, the better it
sounds."[29]

ADAM'S HISTORICAL ROLE

        Overall, Adam cannot be considered to be a great com-
poser, that is, a composer of the first rank. He is not of
the stature of Wagner or Verdi in opera nor of Tchaikovsky
or Delibes in ballet. But neither is he a hack or inferior
talent as is sometimes suggested. The fairest appraisal is
that he is a musician of the second or third rank, one with
considerable artistic ability which was not utilized fully
or consistently. In spite of his deficiencies, he produced
some creditable enduring pieces of music, a few of which,
notably **Cantique de Noël** and **Giselle,** are better known than
their creator.

        Besides the several works which are still appreci-
ated today, he is a historical personage with a two-pronged
contribution to the stream of music. In opera he was one of
the key figures in the development of light opera, a major
link in the genre which evolved into twentieth century
musical comedy.[30] In ballet he was the apparent precursor
of Léo Delibes, the father of modern ballet music. Accord-
ingly, he has the distinction of earning two meaningful

historical honors, one as an important ancestor of the
Broadway stage, the other, in a sense, as the "grandfather
of modern ballet music."

NOTES

(The numbers refer to the items in the bibliography)

1. Item 19.

2. See items 395-402.

3. For more information on his life and works, see his
    major biography (items 40 and 41) or the better
    reference articles on him (for example, items 14, 18,
    19, 24, 30, and 36).

4. See items 2-5.

5. This friendship is reflected in Adam's essay on
    Boieldieu's professorship (item 1).

6. For a more detailed analysis of Adam's influence on
    Delibes' ballets, see item 66.

7. Item 40.

8. Item 16.

9. Item 11.

10. Item 20.

11. Item 189.

12. Item 188.

13. Item 18.

14. Item 19.

15. Item 69.

16. Item 137.

17. Item 56.

18. See item 189.

19. Item 30.

20. Item 24.

21. See items 327, 332, 346, 353, 356, and 357.

22. See items 378, 380, 381, 384, 385, 386, 387, and 388.

23. See item 377.

24. See item 254.

25. See items 266, 267, 268, and 269.

26. See item 286, the item following 286, the item following 291, the item following 293, the section on movies under **Le corsaire,** and the section on **Celebration.**

27. Item 24.

28. Item 189.

29. Item 124.

30. See item 308.

MUSICAL WORKS

BALLETS

(Unless otherwise indicated, all first
performed in Paris)

1. **La chatte blanche**

    July 26, 1830, Nouveautés, in collaboration with
    Casimir Gide.

2. **Faust** (3 acts)

    February 16, 1833, King's Theatre, London;
    scenarist, André Deshayes.

3. **La fille du Danube** (2 acts)

    September 21, 1836, Opéra; scenarists, Fillipo
    Taglioni and Eugène Desmarès.

4. **Les mohicans** (2 acts)

    July 5, 1837, Opéra; scenarist, Antonio Guerra.

5. **Morskoĭ razboĭnik (L'écumeur de mer)** (2 acts)

    February 21, 1840, St. Peterbsurg; the Russian
    title was derived from the title "Morskoĭ
    rasbonick," which was given in one French source
    (bibliography item 40).

6. **Die Hamadryaden** (2 act opera-ballet)

    April 28, 1840, Court Opera, Berlin; scenarist,
    Théodore Pernot de Colombey.

7. **Giselle, ou, Les Wilis** (2 acts)

    June 28, 1841, Opéra; scenarists, Jules Henri
    Vernoy de Saint-Georges and Théophile Gautier;
    some sources indicate that Jean Coralli also
    collaborated on the scenario.

8. **La jolie fille de Gand** (3 acts)

    June 22, 1842, Opéra; scenarists, Jules Henri
    Vernoy de Saint-Georges and Albert [François
    Decombe]; later presented in a variation,
    Beatrice di Gand, ovvero, Un sogno.

15

9.   **Le diable à quatre** (2 acts)

> August 11, 1845, Opéra; scenarists, Adolphe de
> Leuven and Joseph Mazilier.

10. **The Marble Maiden** (3 acts)

> September 27, 1845, Drury Lane, London;
> scenarists Jules Henri Vernoy de Saint-Georges
> and Albert [François Decombe].

11. **Griseldis, ou, Les cinq sens (Grisélidis)** (3 acts)

> February 16, 1848, Opéra; scenarists, Philippe
> François Pinel Dumanoir and Joseph Mazilier.

12. **La filleule des fées** (3 acts and a prologue)

> October 8, 1849, Opéra, in collaboration with
> Clémenceau de Saint-Julien; scenarists, Jules
> Henri Vernoy de Saint-Georges and Jules Perrot.

13. **Orfa** (2 acts)

> December 29, 1852, Opéra; scenarists, Henry
> Trianon and Joseph Mazilier.

14. **Rilla** (1? act and a prologue)

> Performed 1855-56 at the Carnevale, La Scala,
> Milan, with music by Adam and Jean Baptiste
> Rochefort; scenarist, Lucien Petipa.

15. **Le corsaire** (2 acts)

> January 23, 1856, Opéra; scenarists, Jules Henri
> Vernoy de Saint-Georges and Joseph Mazilier.

OPERATIC WORKS

(Unless otherwise indicated, all
first performed in Paris)

1.   **Pierre et Marie, ou, Le soldat ménétrier** (1 act
vaudeville)

> January 22, 1824, Gymnase.

2.   **Le baiser au porteur** (1 act vaudeville)

> June 9, 1824, Gymnase.

3. **Le bal champêtre** (1 act vaudeville)

    October 21, 1824, Gymnase.

4. **La haine d'une femme** (1 act vaudeville)

    December 14, 1824, Gymnase.

5. **L'exilé** (2 act vaudeville)

    July 9, 1825, Vaudeville.

6. **La dame jaune** (1 act vaudeville)

    March 7, 1826, Vaudeville; librettists, Pierre
    François Adolphe Carmouche and Édouard Joseph
    Mazères.

7. **L'oncle d'Amérique** (1 act vaudeville)

    March 14, 1826, Gymnase; librettists, Augustin
    Eugène Scribe and Édouard Joseph Mazères.

8. **L'anonyme** (2 act vaudeville)

    May 29, 1826, Vaudeville; librettists, Armand
    François Jouslin de La Salle, Charles Désiré
    Dupeuty, and Théodore Ferdinand Vallon de
    Villeneuve.

9. **Le hussard de Felsheim** (3 act vaudeville)

    March 9, 1827, Vaudeville; librettists, Charles
    Désiré Dupeuty, Théodore Ferdinand Vallon de
    Villeneuve, and Amable Vilain de Saint-Hilaire.

10. **L'héritière et l'orpheline** (2 act vaudeville)

    May 12, 1827, Vaudeville; librettists, Théodore
    Anne and Jules Henri de Tully.

11. **Perkins Warbeck, ou, Le commis marchand** (2 act
    vaudeville)

    May 15, 1827, Gymnase; librettists, Marie
    Emmanuel Théaulon de Lambert, Nicholas Brazier,
    and Pierre François Adolphe Carmouche.

12. **Mon ami Pierre** (1 act vaudeville)

    September 8, 1827, Nouveautés; librettist,
    Armand d'Artois.

13. **Monsieur Botte** (3 act vaudeville)

>   November 15, 1827, Vaudeville; librettists,
>   Charles Désiré Dupeuty and Théodore Ferdinand
>   Vallon de Villeneuve.

14. **Le Caleb de Walter Scott** (1 act vaudeville)

>   December 12, 1827, Nouveautés; librettists,
>   Armand d'Artois and François Antoine Eugène
>   de Planard; about one-third of the music was by
>   Adam.

15. **Le mal du pays, ou, La batelière de Brientz**
     (1 act vaudeville)

>   December 28, 1827, Gymnase; librettists
>   Augustin Eugène Scribe and Mélesville [Anne
>   Honoré Joseph Duveyrier].

16. **Lidda, ou, La jeune servante** (1 act vaudeville)

>   January 16, 1828, Nouveautés; librettist,
>   Théodore Anne.

17. **La reine de seize ans** (2 act vaudeville)

>   January 30, 1828, Gymnase; librettist, Jean
>   François Alfred Bayard.

18. **La barbier chatêlain, ou, La loterie de Francfort**
     (3 act vaudeville)

>   February 7, 1828, Nouveautés; librettists,
>   Théodore Anne and Marie Emmanuel Théaulon de
>   Lambert.

19. **Les comediens par testament** (1 act vaudeville)

>   April 14, 1828, Nouveautés; librettists, Louis
>   Benoit Picard and Jean Baptiste Pierre Lafitte.

20. **Les trois cantons, ou, La Confédération suisse**
     (3 act vaudeville)

>   June 16, 1828, Vaudeville; librettists, Théodore
>   Ferdinand Vallon de Villeneuve and Charles
>   Désiré Dupeuty.

21.   **Valentine, ou, La chute des feuilles**
        (2 act vaudeville)

> October 2, 1828, Nouveautés; librettists, Amable
> Vilain de Saint- Hilaire and Théodore Ferdinand
> Vallon de Villeneuve.

22.   **Le clé** (3 act vaudeville)

> November 5, 1828, Vaudeville; librettists, Marie
> François Denis Thérésa Leroi, Baron d'Allarde,
> and Hyppolyte [Hippolyte Lucas?]

23.   **Le jeune propriétaire et la vieux fermier, ou,**
        La ville et le village (3 act vaudeville)

> February 6, 1829, Nouveautés; librettist,
> Armand d'Artois.

24.   **Pierre et Catherine** (2 act opéra comique)

> February 9, 1829, Opéra-Comique; librettist,
> Jules Henri Vernoy de Saint-Georges.

25.   **Isaure** (3 act vaudeville)

> October 1, 1829, Nouveautés.

26.   **Henri V et ses compagnons** (3 act pasticcio)

> February 27, 1830, Nouveautés.

27.   **Danilowa** (3 act opéra comique)

> April 23, 1830, Opéra-Comique; librettists,
> Jean Baptiste Vial and Nicolas Paul Duport.

28.   **Rafaël** (3 act pasticcio)

> April 26, 1830, Nouveautés.

29.   **Trois jours en une heure** (1 act opéra comique)

> August 21, 1830, Opéra-Comique, in collaboration
> with Henri Romagnesi; librettists, Gabriel [Jules
> Joseph Gabriel de Lurieu] and Michel Masson.

30.   **Les trois Catherine** (3 act vaudeville)

> November 18, 1830, Nouveautés, in collaboration
> with Casimir Gide.

31. **Joséphine, ou, Le retour de Wagram** (1 act
     opéra comique)

> December 2, 1830, Opéra-Comique; librettists,
> Gabriel [Jules Joseph Gabriel de Lurieu], and
> Ferdinand Delaboullaye.

32. **Le morceau d'ensemble** (1 act opéra comique)

> March 7, 1831, Opéra-Comique; librettists,
> Pierre François Adolphe Carmouche and Frédéric
> de Courcy.

33. **Le grand prix, ou, Le voyage à frais communs**
     (3 act opéra comique)

> July 9, 1831, Opéra-Comique; librettists, Gabriel
> [Jules Joseph Gabriel de Lurieu], and Michel
> Masson.

34. **Casimir, ou, Le premier tête à tête** (2 act vaudeville)

> December 1, 1831, Nouveautés.

35. **His First Campaign (The First Campaign)**
     (2 act military spectacle)

> October 1, 1832, Covent Garden, London.

36. **The Dark Diamond** (3 act historical melodrama)

> November 5, 1832, Covent Garden, London.

37. **Le proscrit, ou, Le tribunal invisible** (3 act
     opéra comique)

> September 18, 1833, Opéra-Comique; librettists,
> Pierre Françoise Adolphe Carmouche, and Joseph
> Xavier Boniface Saintine.

38. **Une bonne fortune** (1 act opéra comique)

> January 23, 1834, Opéra-Comique; librettists,
> Féréol [Louis Henri Felix Second] and Édouard
> [Édouard Damarin].

39. **Le chalet** (1 act opéra comique)

> September 25, 1834, Opéra-Comique; librettists,
> Augustin Eugène Scribe and Mélesville [Anne
> Honoré Joseph Duveyrier].

40.   **La marquise** (1 act opéra comique)

> February 28, 1835, Opéra-Comique; librettists,
> Jules Henri Vernoy de Saint-Georges and Adolphe
> de Leuven.

41.   **Micheline, ou, L'heure d'esprit** (1 act opéra comique)

> June 29, 1835, Opéra-Comique; librettists,
> Amable Vilain de Saint-Hilaire, Michel Masson,
> and Théodore Ferdinand Vallon de Villeneuve.

42.   **Le postillon de Lonjumeau (Le postillon de Longjumeau)**
      (3 act opéra comique)

> October 13, 1836, Opéra-Comique; librettists,
> Adolphe de Leuven and Brunswick [Léon Lévy
> Lhérie].

43.   **Le fidèle berger** (3 act opéra comique)

> January 6, 1838, Opéra-Comique; librettists,
> Augustin Eugène Scribe and Jules Henri Vernoy
> de Saint-Georges.

44.   **Le brasseur de Preston** (3 act opéra comique)

> October 31, 1838, Opéra-Comique; librettists,
> Adolphe de Leuven and Brunswick [Léon Lévy
> Lhérie].

45.   **Regine, ou, Les deux nuits** (2 act opéra comique)

> January 17, 1839, Opéra-Comique; librettist,
> Augustin Eugène Scribe.

46.   **La reine d'un jour** (3 act opéra comique)

> September 19, 1839, Opéra-Comique; librettists,
> Augustin Eugène Scribe and Jules Henri Vernoy
> de Saint-Georges.

47.   **La rose de Péronne** (3 act opéra comique)

> December 12, 1840, Opéra-Comique; librettists,
> Adolphe de Leuven and Adolphe Philippe D'Ennery
> [Adolphe Philippe].

48.   **La main de fer, ou, Le mariage secret** (3 act
      opéra comique)

> October 26, 1841, Opéra–Comique; librettists,
> Augustin Eugène Scribe and Adolphe de Leuven.

49.   **La roi d'Yvetot** (3 act opéra comique)

> October 13, 1842, Opéra–Comique; librettists,
> Adolphe de Leuven and Brunswick [Léon Lévy
> Lhérie].

50.   **Lambert Simnel** (3 act opéra comique)

> September 14, 1843, Opéra–Comique; librettists,
> Augustin Eugène Scribe and Mélesville [Anne
> Honoré Joseph Duveyrier]; work begun by
> Hippolyte Monpou, and completed by Adam.

51.   **Cagliostro** (3 act opéra comique)

> February 10, 1844, Opéra–Comique; librettists,
> Augustin Eugène Scribe and Jules Henri Vernoy
> de Saint–Georges.

52.   **Richard en Palestine** (3 act opéra)

> October 7, 1844, Opéra; librettist, Paul Henri
> Foucher.

53.   **La bouquetière** (1 act opera)

> May 31, 1847, Opéra; librettist, Hippolyte Lucas.

54.   **Les premiers pas** (1 act prologue)

> November 15, 1847, Opéra–National, in collabo-
> ration with Daniel Auber, Michele Carafa, and
> Jacques François Fromental Halévy; librettists,
> Alphonse Royer and Gustave Vaëz [Jean Nicholas
> Gustave van Nieuwenhuysen].

55.   **Le toréador, ou, L'accord parfait** (2 act
      opéra comique)

> May 18, 1849, Opéra–Comique; librettist, Thomas
> Marie François Sauvage.

56.   **Le fanal** (2 act opera)

> December 24, 1849, Opéra; librettist, Jules Henri
> Vernoy de Saint–Georges.

57.   **Giralda, ou, La nouvelle Psyché** (3 act opéra comique)

> July 20, 1850, Opéra-Comique; librettist,
> Augustin Eugène Scribe.

58.   **La poupée de Nuremberg** (1 act opéra comique)

> February 21, 1852, Opéra-National; librettists,
> Adolphe de Leuven and Victor Arthur Rousseau de
> Beauplan.

59.   **La farfadet** (1 act opéra comique)

> March 19, 1852, Opéra-Comique; librettist,
> François Antoine Eugène de Planard.

60.   **Si j'étais roi** (3 act opéra comique)

> September 4, 1852, Théâtre-Lyrique; librettists,
> Adolphe Philippe D'Ennery [Adolphe Philippe]
> and Jules Brésil.

61.   **La faridondaine** (5 act drama with songs)

> December 30, 1852, Porte Saint-Martin, in
> collaboration with A. De Groot; librettists,
> Charles Desiré Dupeuty and Ernest Bourget.

62.   **Le sourd, ou, L'auberge pleine** (3 act opéra comique)

> February 2, 1853, Opéra-Comique; librettists,
> Joseph Adolphe Ferdinand Langlé and Adolphe de
> Leuven, after Pierre Jean Baptiste Choudard
> Desforges.

63.   **Le roi des halles** (3 act opéra comique)

> April 11, 1853, Théâtre-Lyrique; librettists,
> Adolphe de Leuven and Brunswick [Léon Lévy Lhérie].

64.   **Le bijou perdu** (3 act opéra comique)

> October 6, 1853, Théâtre-Lyrique; librettists,
> Adolphe de Leuven and P.A.A. Pittaud de Forges.

65.   **Le muletier de Tolède** (3 act opéra comique)

> December 16, 1854, Théâtre-Lyrique; librettists,
> Adolphe Philippe D'Ennery [Adolphe Philippe]
> and Louis François Nicholaie Clairville.

66. **À Clichy** (1 act opéra comique)

>December 24, 1854, Théâtre-Lyrique; librettists,
>Adolphe Philippe D'Ennery [Adolphe Philippe] and
>Eugène Grangé [Eugène Pierre Basté].

67. **Le houzard de Berchini (Le housard de Berchini;
Le hussard de Berchini)** (2 act opéra comique)

>October 17, 1855, Opéra-Comique; librettist,
>Joseph Bernard Rosier.

68. **Falstaff** (1 act opéra comique)

>January 18, 1856, Théâtre-Lyrique; librettists,
>Jules Henri Vernoy de Saint-Georges and Adolphe
>de Leuven, after William Shakespeare.

69. **Mam'zelle Geneviève** (2 act opéra comique)

>March 24, 1856, Théâtre-Lyrique; librettists,
>Brunswick [Léon Lévy Lhérie] and Victor Arthur
>Rousseau de Beauplan.

70. **Les pantins de Violette** (1 act operetta)

>April 29, 1856, Bouffes-Parisiens; librettist,
>Léon Battu.

71. **La dernier bal** (3 act opéra comique)

>Completed just before Adam's death but not per-
>formed or published; the libretto may have been
>by Augustin Eugène Scribe.

CANTATAS

(All definitely first performed in Paris,
except for 1 and 2, which were probably first
performed in Paris).

1. **Agnès Sorel**

>1824; lyrics by Viellard.

2. **Ariane à Naxos**

>1825; lyrics by J.A. Vinaty.

3. **Les nations**

> August 6, 1851, Opéra; lyrics by Théodore
> de Banville.

4. **La fête des arts**

> November 16, 1852, Opéra-Comique; lyrics by
> Joseph Méry.

5. **Victoire**

> September 13, 1855, Opéra-Comique and Théâtre-
> Lyrique; lyrics by Michel Carré.

6. [Unnamed cantata]

> March 17, 1856, Opéra; lyrics by Emilien Pacini.

RELIGIOUS MUSIC

1. **Messe solennelle** (four solo voices, chorus and
   various instruments)

> March 26, 1837, Saint-Eustache Church, Paris.

2. **Cantique de Noël (Minuit, chrétiens; Noël)**
   (solo carol)

> December, 1847, Roquemaure, France; lyrics by
> Placide Cappeau.

3. **Messe de Saint-Cecile** (solo voices, chorus and
   orchestra)

> November 22, 1850.

4. **Messe de l'orphéon** (four male voices and orchestra)

> April 26, 1851, Cathedral of Meaux, France, in col-
> laboration with Jacques François Fromental Halévy,
> Antoine Louis Clapisson, and Ambroise Thomas.

5. **Mois de Marie de Saint-Philippe** (eight motets with
   organ accompaniment)

> Performed no later than 1855.

6. **Domine salvum** (three voices and chorus with organ
   accompaniment)

> Undated.

7. **Grande marche religieuse de L'Annonciation**
     Undated.

8. **Hymn à la vierge** (solo with organ accompaniment)
     Undated.

9. **Messe à trois voix**
     Undated, in collaboration with Clemenceau de
     Saint-Julien.

10. **O salutaris** (two voices)
     Undated.

11. **O salutaris** (voices, organ, and orchestra)
     Undated.

MISCELLANEOUS COMPOSITIONS

1. Assisted François Boieldieu in the composition of
    La dame blanche (1825).

2. **Les enfants de Paris** (four male voice secular choral
    work without accompaniment)
     1848.

3. **La garde mobile** (four male voice secular choral work
    without accompaniment)
     1848.

4. **La marche républicaine** (four male voice secular choral
    work with orchestra)
     1848.

5. **Les métiers** (four male voice secular choral work)
     Undated.

6. **La muette** (four male voice secular choral work
    without accompaniment)
     Undated.

7. **Grande sonate** (piano, violin, and violincello)
     Undated.

8. Songs/minor vocal pieces (at least 65)

9. Piano music (about 200 light works)

10. Harmonium music (at least 7 pieces)

11. Military music (some military-style arrangements plus a military march first performed November 15, 1840)

ARRANGEMENTS AND REORCHESTRATIONS OF THEATRICAL WORKS BY OTHERS

1. Grétry, André. **Richard Coeur–de–lion.**

2. _____ . **Zémire et Azor.**

3. Monsigny, Pierre. **Félix.**

4. _____ . **Aline.**

5. _____ . **Le déserteur.**

6. Dalayrac, Nicolas. **Gulistan.**

7. Solié, Jean Pierre. **Le diable à quatre.**

8. Isouard, Nicolas. **Cendrillon.**

9. Donizetti, Gaetano. **Betly.**

> Arrangement presented December 27, 1853 at the Opéra, Paris.

WORKS DERIVED FROM ADAM'S MUSIC

1. **Katerina** (3 act ballet)

> May 25, 1935, Kirov Theater, Leningrad; scenarist, Leonid Lavrovski; most of the music was by Anton Rubinstein, with the music of the serf's ballet by Adam.

2. **Giselle's Revenge** (ballet)

> November 22, 1953, Henry Street Playhouse, New York; a parody of **Giselle**, with music from that ballet.

3. **Pas de Deux for Four** (ballet)

    February 6, 1967, Theater 80 St. Marks Place,
    New York; the music was from **Le diable à quatre.**

4. **Celebration** (ballet)

    June 29, 1973, Teatro Nuovo, Spoleto, Italy;
    ten pas de deux (including the pas de deux from
    Le corsaire) plus a prologue and epilogue.

5. **L'air d'esprit** (ballet)

    February 7-19, 1978, Auditorium Theater, Chicago;
    a pas de deux with music written for **Giselle** but
    not used in its score.

6. **Le jardin animé** (ballet)

    May 20, 1981, Metropolitan Opera House, New York;
    the music was by Léo Delibes, Adam (from
    Le corsaire) and Riccardo Drigo.

BIBLIOGRAPHY

ADAM'S WRITINGS

1. Adam, Adolphe. "Une classe de piano sous le Consulat." **Vie musical** 9 (1968): 15-17.

    Well-written essay on Boieldieu's piano class at the Conservatory during the period from 1799 to 1804. Adam is very complimentary to the professorship of his chief teacher and friend.

2. ———. **Derniers souvenirs d'un musicien.** Paris: Lévy, 1859.
    ML 390.A19

    Volume two of Adam's memoirs. It is perhaps not quite as well done as the first volume, but is still good, lively reading. Other editions were published in 1871 and in the 1880's.

3. ———. "Lettres sur la musique française, 1836–1850." **La revue de Paris** 10 (August–September, 1903).

    In four parts (August, pp. 449–481 and 726–762; September, pp. 137–176 and 275–320); well-written letters of Adam to Spiker, a Berlin librarian under Frederick William III and Frederick William IV. In addition to providing valuable autobiographical material, the letters give Adam's views on the music and musicians of the period.

4. ———. "The Musicans of Paris: Thoughts on Their Place in Life by the composer of Giselle." **Musical America** 70 (May 1950): 8, 42

    Translation of an essay by Adam on the musicians of Paris as a generic composite. Spritely, witty, and very competently written, the essay is highly recommended reading as a key to understanding Adam's psychology and his ability as a writer.

5. ———. **Souvenirs d'un Musicien.** Paris: Lévy, 1857.
    ML 390.A18

Volume one of Adam's memoirs. Skillfully written
and quite interesting in content, this work is Adam's
most important piece of writing and one of the more
readable memoirs of any composer. Indicative of its
value are the various reprints which have been produced (1860, 1868, 1884, and another in the 1880's).

GENERAL WORKS ON ADAM

6. Albrecht, Otto E. **A Census of Autograph Music
    Manuscripts of European Composers in American
    Libraries.** Philadelphia: University of
    Pennsylvania Press, 1953, pp. 1-2.
    ML 135.A2   A4

    Four items of Adam's are given on this list of com-
    posers' manuscripts in United States libraries. Des-
    cription and location of each item are provided.

7. Aubayet, Xavier. **Les jugements nouveau.** Paris:
    Librairie nouvelle, 1860.

    Contains commentary on Adam by a contemporary.

8. Barzun, Jacques. **Berlioz and the Romantic Century.**
    3d ed. 2 vols. New York: Columbia University
    Press, 1969.
    ML 410.B5   B2   1969

    Has a fair amount of material on the relationship/
    interface between Adam and Berlioz. Other biographies
    of Berlioz usually have some material on Adam.

9. Clément, Félix. **Les musiciens célèbres.** Paris:
    Hachette, 1868.

    Includes a biographical sketch on Adam which is
    overly and perhaps unfairly negative.

10. Cross, Milton, and David Ewen. **Encyclopedia of the
    Great Composers and Their Music.** New rev. ed.
    Garden City, N.Y.: Doubleday, 1962, vol. 1, p. 425.
    ML 385.C7   1962

    Of interest because of the anecdote concerning
    Adam's music. When Edouard Lalo was reportedly ad-
    vised to emulate Adam, Lalo's response, supposedly,
    was that he was not interested in concocting bonbons.

11. Curzon, Henri de. "Adam (Adolphe-Charles)." **Diction-
    naire de biographie française.** Edited by J.

Balteau and others. Paris: Librairie Letouzey et
ané, 1933–, vol. 1, pp. 429–31.
CT 143.D5

Standard French reference article. The author's
opinion of Adam's music is generally negative,
including the comments "essentially superficial" and
"one sees there too constantly that this excellent
musician was never an artist."

12. Debay, V., and P. Locard. "Adam (Adolphe–Charles)."
**Encyclopédie de la musique et dictionnaire du
Conservatoire.** Edited by Albert Lavignac and
Lionel de la Laurencie. Paris: C. Delagrave,
1913–31, pt. 1, vol. 3, pp. 1676–77.
ML 100.E5

Good French reference article. There is no bibliography or list of works, but another article in the
same work (item 36) has both.

13. Denne–Baron, Dieudonné. "Adam (Adolphe–Charles)."
**Nouvelle biographie générale depuis les temps le
plus reculés jusqu'à nos jours.** Edited by Jean
Hoefer. Paris: Didot Frères, 1853–66, vol. 1,
pp. 222–25.
CT 143.H5

Comprehensive contemporary reference essay on Adam,
with the period up to about 1850 covered.

14. Dumesnil, René. **La musique romantique française.**
Paris: Aubier, 1944, pp. 130–39.
ML 270.D85

Very good overview of Adam and his works, with
individual sections/paragraphs on **Le chalet, Le postillon de Lonjumeau, Le toréador, Giselle, Giralda,
Si j'étais roi, La poupée de Nuremberg,** and **Cantique
de Noël.**

15. Escudier, Léon. **Mes souvenirs.** Paris: Dentu, 1863.

Escudier's memoirs, including material on Adam.

16. Evans, Edwin. "The Composer of Giselle." **Dancing
Times,** no. 350 (November 1939): 63–65

Very provocative essay on Adam. The author's view
of Adam's music is definitely negative. He states,
concerning **Giselle,** that the "survival of the ballet

is due to the dancers, not to the music." He also
claims that with a few exceptions, "oblivion has over-
taken the composer." In reference to Adam's artistic
characteristics, he declares that "these are not the
qualities that lead to immortality." The most valuable part of the article is the appreciable amount of
space devoted to describing Adam's trip to Russia and
Germany in 1839–1840.

17. _____. **Music and the Dance, for Lovers of the
     Ballet.** London: H. Jenkins, 1948, pp. 116–18.
     ML 3460.E9

     Same basic essay as item 16.

18. Ewen, David. **Great Composers, 1300–1900: A Biograph-
     ical and Critical Guide.** New York: H.W. Wilson,
     1966, pp. 9–10.
     ML 105.E944

     Good general reference article. The author thinks
     well enough of Adam to include him in a work on great
     composers, but admits that "what he lacked most were
     dramatic power, emotional depth, and genuine creative
     originality."

19. _____. **The Lighter Classics in Music: A Compre-
     hensive Guide to Musical Masterworks in a Lighter
     Vein by 187 Composers.** New York: Arco, 1961,
     pp. 2–4.
     MT 6.E9

     Well-done short essay on Adam and his works. Al-
     though covering all of Adam's important compositions,
     the essay's emphasis is on **Giselle** and **Si j'étais roi.**
     The writer describes Adam as "a master of expressive
     and dramatized melodies," and an "eminent composer of
     of comic operas."

20. Fétis, François Joseph. **Biographie universelle des
     musiciens et bibliographie générale de la musique.**
     2d ed. Paris: Didot Frères, 1873–75, vol. 1,
     pp. 14–17.
     ML 105.F42

     One of the best 19th-century reference articles on
     Adam. The terms "jolies mélodies" and "gracieuses
     bagatelles" are used to describe Adam's music. This
     8 volume work had many other editions.

21.   _____ . **Biographie universelle des musiciens et
       Bibliographie générale de la musique.** 2d ed.
       Brussels: Culture et civilization, 1963, vol. 1,
       pp. 14–17.
       ML 105.F42 1963

       Reprint of item 20.

22.   _____ . **Biographie universelle des musiciens et
       Bibliographie générale de la musique: Supplément
       et complément.** Edited by Arthur Pougin. Paris:
       Didot, 1878–80, vol. 1, p. 6.
       ML 105.F422

       Supplement to item 20, principally a listing of
       additional works.

23.   _____ . **Biographie universelle des musiciens et
       Bibliographie générale de la musique: Supplément
       et complément.** Edited by Arthur Pougin. Brussels:
       Culture and civilization, 1963, vol. 1, p. 6.
       ML 105.F422 1963

       Reprint of item 22.

24.   Forbes, Elizabeth. "Adam, Adolphe (Charles)."
       The New Grove Dictionary of Music and Musicians.
       Edited by Stanley Sadie. London: Macmillan, 1980,
       vol. 1, pp. 90–93.
       ML 100.N48   ISBN 0333231112

       Perhaps the best reference article on Adam. The
       author is very favorable to Adam's music, describing
       it as "graceful and charming" and "eminently danceable
       music." She further states that several of Adam's
       operas and ballets have "scores full of genuine inspi-
       ation," and that Adam had "a sense of the theater."
       The list of Adam's works is excellent, but the bibli-
       ography is barely adequate.

25.   Halévy, Jacques François Fromental. **Discours prononcé
       aux funérailles de Adolphe Adam.** Paris: Didot,
       1856.

       Funeral address given at the Institut Impérial de
       France, May 5, 1856.

26.   _____ . "Notice sur la vie et les ouvrages de
       M. Adolphe Adam." **Academie des beaux-arts, Paris:
       Annuaire, 1859.** Paris: Didot, 1859.

Commemorative essay on Adam by a friend. The exact
citation is uncertain. The essay was also published
in item 27.

27.   _____ . **Souvenirs et portraits: Etudes sur les
            beaux-arts.** Paris: Lévy, 1861.
            ML 60.H19

            Contains same essay as item 26.

28.   Harding, James. **Jacques Offenbach: A Biography.**
            London: J. Calder, 1980, pp. 45–47.
            ML 410.041 H37   ISBN 0714538353

            Has some good material on the relationship/interface
            between Offenbach and Adam. In addition, there is
            some valuable personal data on Adam, including his
            affinity for England and the monument which was raised
            in his honor by the citizens of Longjumeau. Other
            biographies of Offenbach usually have some material on
            Adam.

29.   Huart, Louis. **Galerie de la presse, de la littérature
            et des beaux-arts.** Paris: Au bureau de la publi-
            cation, et Chez Aubert, 1839–1841, vol. 1.
            CT 1012.H8

            Contains material on Adam by a contemporary.

30.   Hueffer, Francis. "Adam, Adolphe (Charles)." **Grove's
            Dictionary of Music and Musicians.** 5th ed. Edited
            by Eric Blom. New York: St. Martin's, 1954–1961,
            vol. 1, pp. 47–49.
            ML 100.G885 1954

            Good general reference article. Although overall
            favorable to Adam's music, the author states that
            Adam's artistic style was "frequently fatal to his
            higher aspirations."

31.   Kloppenburg, W.C.M. "Adolphe Charles Adam (1803–1856)."
            Mens en melodie 11 (April 1956): 100–04.

            Commemorative article on Adam on the occasion of the
            centennial of his death. This is a good example of
            appreciation of Adam after the passage of a century.

32.   Labat-Poussin, Brigitte, ed. **Archives du Théâtre
            national de 1'Opéra: AJ13 1 à 1466: Inventaire.**
            Paris: Archives nationales, 1977.
            ML 136.P2 058   ISBN 286000016X

Inventory of the archives of the Paris Opéra, containing 17 citations for Adam. The indexes are excellent.

33. Lajarte, Théodore de, ed. **Bibliothèque musicale du Théâtre de l'Opéra: Catalogue historique, chronologique, anecdotique.** 2 vols. Paris: Librairie des bibliophiles, 1878.
     ML 136.P2 O6

     Presents the repertory of the Paris Opéra from 1671 to 1876, including material on Adam's work.

34. ———— . **Bibliothèque musicale du Théâtre de l'Opéra: Catalogue historique, chronologique, anecdotique.** 2 vols. Hildesheim: G. Olms, 1969.

     Reprint of item 33.

35. Lalo, Pierre. **De Rameau à Ravel: Portraits et souvenirs.** Paris: A. Michel, 1947, pp. 313-22.
     ML 385.L35

     Description of and commentary on Adam's 1836-1850 correspondence with a Berliner named Spiker. See item 3 for the actual correspondence.

36. Landormy, Paul, and Joseph Loisel. "Adam." **Encyclopédie de la musique et dictionaire du conservatoire.** Edited by Albert Lavignac and Lionel de la Laurencie. Paris: C. Delagrave, 1913-1931, pt. 2, vol. 6, pp. 3495-3497.
     ML 100.E5

     Good standard French reference article, with an excellent list of works and a short bibliography.

37. Lardin, Jules. **Zémire et Azor par Grétry: Quelques questions à propos de la nouvelle falsification de cet opéra.** Paris: Impr. d'A. Moessard et Jousset, 1846.

     On Grétry's opera, with some material on Adam (who made a reorchestration of the work).

38. Mirecourt, Eugène de [Charles Jacquot]. **Arnal, Adolphe Adam.** Paris: Faure, 1868.

     Although this biography of Adam is short and ordinary, it is the first known one in French. The other biographee is the French comedian Etienne Arnal.

39.   Neumann, William. **Adrien François Boieldieu, Adolph**
        Adam: Biographien. Kassel: E. Balde 1855. 140 p.

        Moderate-sized sketches of the two composers, the one on
      Adam being the earliest known biography.

40.   Pougin, Arthur. **Adolphe Adam: Sa vie, sa carrière,**
        ses memoires artistiques. Paris: Charpentier,
        1877. 370 p.
      ML 410.A19 P8

        Only comprehensive treatise on Adam's life and
      works. A well-done book, very sympathetic to Adam,
      with: considerable biographical information; exten-
      sive exposition on his works (including the lesser
      known ones); comprehensive listings of his works,
      including his religious music, songs, piano music, and
      miscellaneous other compositions; commentary on Adam
      as a literary author; and a good sample of his criti-
      cisms of contemporary composers.

41.   ———— . **Adolphe Adam: Sa vie, sa carrière, ses**
        memoires artistiques. Geneva: Minkoff reprint,
        1973. 371 p.
      ML 410.A19 P8 1973   ISBN 2826600397

        Reprint of item 40.

42.   Prod'homme, Jacques Gabriel. **L'Opéra, 1669–1925.**
        Paris: Delagrave, 1925.
      ML 1727.8.P2 P8

        History of the Paris Opéra, including the chrono-
      logical record of its repertory. There is some data
      on Adam's works.

43.   Turner, J. Righbie. "Nineteenth-century Autograph
        Music Manuscripts in the Pierpont Morgan Library."
        Nineteenth Century Music 4, no. 1 (1980): 54.

        Contains information on two of Adam's manuscripts.

                    ADAM'S BALLETS IN GENERAL

44.   **L'art du ballet des origines à nos jours.** Paris:
        Editions du tambourinaire, 1952.

        Very good collection of essays on the history of
      the ballet, including coverage of several of Adam's
      ballets.

45.   Arvey, Verna. **Choreographic Music: Music for the Dance.** New York: Dutton, 1941, pp. 89-90.
        ML 3400.A78

        Short but worthwhile material on Adam's ballets in one of the better books on dance music.

46.   Chujoy, Anatole, and Phyllis Winifred Manchester, eds. **The Dance Encyclopedia.** Rev. and enlarged ed. New York: Simon and Schuster, 1967.
        GV 1585.C5 1967

        This comprehensive reference book on dance has essays on Adam and some of his ballets. Another edition was published in 1949 by A.S. Barnes, New York.

47.   Clarke, Mary, and Clement Crisp. **Design for Ballet.** London: Studio Vista, 1978.
        GV 1782.C56   ISBN 0289705967

        Excellent monograph on design of ballet sets and costumes with some material on Adam's ballets. Another edition was published in 1978 by Hawthorn Books, New York.

48.   Clarke, Mary, and David Vaughan, eds. **The Encyclopedia of Dance & Ballet.** London: Pitman, 1977.
        GV 1585.E53   ISBN 0273010883

        This comprehensive reference book on the dance has essays on Adam and some of his ballets. Another edition was published in 1977 by Putnam, New York.

49.   Guest, Ivor. **Le ballet de l'Opéra de Paris: Trois siècles d'histoire et de tradition.** Translation by Paul Alexandre. Paris: Théâtre national de l'Opéra, 1976.
        GV 1787.G8

        Excellent history of the Paris Opéra's presentation of ballets, including several of Adam's ballets.

50.   _____ . **Fanny Elssler.** London: Black, 1970.
        GV 1785.E4 G8 1970b   ISBN 0713610611

        Biography of the ballerina, including material on several of Adam's ballets. Another edition was published by Wesleyan University Press in 1970.

51.   _____ . **The Romantic Ballet in Paris.** London:
            Pitman, 1966.
        GV 1650.P3 G8 1966a

        This fine history of Parisian ballet from 1820 to
        1847 has some material on Adam's ballets. Another
        edition was published by Wesleyan University Press in
        1966.

52.   Haskell, Arnold L., ed. **The Ballet Annual: A Record
            and Yearbook of the Ballet.** London: Black,
            1947-63.

        Eighteen very good annuals, some published by
        Macmillan, New York. The last four issues were also
        by Mary Clarke. Some valuable material on Adam's
        ballets is included.

53.   Kochno, Boris. **Le Ballet.** Paris: Hachette, 1954,
            pp. 89-119.
        GV 1649.K6

        Well-done section on romantic ballet containing a
        fair amount on Adam's ballets, including illustrations
        for **Giselle, La filleule des fées, Orfa,** and **Le
        corsaire.**

54.   Koegler, Horst. **The Concise Oxford Dictionary of
            Ballet.** 2d ed. London: Oxford University Press,
            1982.
        GV 1585.K6313 1982   ISBN 0193113252

        This comprehensive reference book has articles on
        Adam and some of his ballets. Another edition was
        published in 1977.

55.   Leslie, Serge. **A Bibliography of the Dance Collection
            of Doris Niles & Serge Leslie.** Edited by Cyril
            Beaumont. 2 vols. London: C.W. Beaumont, 1966-
            68.
        Z 7514.D2 L4   ISBN 0903102560

        An excellent annotated dance bibliography which
        contains a number of items about Adam.

56.   Lifar, Serge. **La musique par la danse, de Lulli à
            Prokofiev.** Paris: R. Laffont, 1955, pp. 110-13.
        ML 3460.L5

        On Adam's ballet music, primarily on **Giselle** and
        on Adam's relationship with and influence on Delibes.

He is more favorable to Adam's music here than he is
in item 137.

57.   Miguel, Parmenia. **The Ballerinas from the Court of
      Louis XIV to Pavlova.** New York: Macmillan, 1972.
      GV 1785.A1 M47

      Biographies of famous ballerinas, with background
      historical material. Several of Adam's ballets are
      covered.

58.   New York Public Library. **Dictionary Catalog of the
      Dance Collection.** 10 vols. Boston: G.K. Hall.
      1974.
      Z 7514.D2 N462 1974   ISBN 0816111243

      Huge, very well-annotated catalog of dance mater-
      ial. It would be difficult to exaggerate the value of
      this work for ballet research. All types of material
      are included: books, articles, audio-visual materials,
      clippings, etc. Films, recordings, illustrations, and
      other nonprint materials are especially well repre-
      sented in quantity and in detail. A wealth of
      historical data is provided. And all of the informa-
      tion is well coordinated by cross references. In the
      case of Adam, there is a large amount of useful and
      accurate information, including data on ballets
      derived from Adam's music. Many of the older and
      rarer items in this bibliography are listed in the
      catalog, including some items not found elsewhere.

59.   ———— . **Bibliographic Guide to Dance.** Boston: G.K.
      Hall, 1976–.
      Z 7514.D2 N462a   ISSN 0360-2737

      Yearly supplements (one or two volumes each year)
      to item 58, with the same exceptional value for
      research as the main set. 1975 is the first year
      covered.

60.   Reyna, Ferdinando. **A Concise History of Ballet.**
      New York: Grosset & Dunlap, 1965.
      GV 1787.R413

      Translation of item 61.

61.   ———— . **Histoire du ballet.** Paris: Éditions A.
      Somogy, 1964.
      GV 1787.R42

General history of ballet with some material on
Adam's ballets.

62.   _____ . **Historia del ballet.** Madrid: Ediciones
       Daimon, Manuel Tamayo, 1965.

       Translation of item 61.

63.   Roslavleva, Natal'ía Petrovna. **Era of the Russian
       Ballet.** New York: Dutton, 1966.
       GV 1787.R675

       History of ballet in Russia, with some information
       on Adam's ballets. Another edition was published in
       1966 by Gollancz, London.

64.   Sitwell, Sacheverell. **The Romantic Ballet from
       Contemporary Prints.** London: Batsford, 1948.
       GV 1787.S5

       Small treatise on romantic ballet with reproduc-
       tions of ballet illustrations. Several of Adam's
       ballets are covered.

65.   Smakov, Genady.   **The Great Russian Dancers.**
       New York: Knopf, 1964.
       GV 1785.A1 S62 1984   ISBN 0294510747

       Biographies of a number of Russian dancers, with
       material on performance of some of Adam's ballets.

66.   Studwell, William E.   "The Choreographic Chain:
       Seventy Years of Ballet Music." **Dance Scope** 10
       (Spring/Summer 1976):   51–55.

       Explores the historical connection between the
       ballet music of Adam, Delibes, Tchaikovsky, and
       Stravinsky, showing the probable direct connection
       between Adam and Delibes, Delibes and Tchaikovsky,
       and Tchaikovsky and Stravinsky.

67.   Swift, Mary Grace. **The Art of the Dance in the
       U.S.S.R.** Notre Dame, Ind.: University of Notre
       Dame Press, 1968.
       GV 1663.S87

       Contains some material on Adam's ballets as
       presented in the Soviet Union.

68.   Swinson, Cyril. **Guidebook to the Ballet.** New York:
        Macmillan, 1961.

        General book on ballet with some material on Adam's
        ballets. Another edition was published in 1960 by
        English Universities Press, London.

69.   Terry, Walter. **The Ballet Companion: A Popular
        Guide for the Ballet-Goer.** New York: Dodd, Mead,
        1968.
        GV 1787.T323

        Has a relatively small amount of space devoted to
        Adam's ballets, but it is very well done. The author
        explains why "Giselle is almost a choreographed score,"
        and describes the music of **Giselle** in a most eloquent
        manner: "Its sounds are marvelous guides to the
        steps, gestures, moods, and dramatic surges of one of
        the greatest dramatic ballets of all time."

70.   Van Praagh, Peggy, and Peter Brinson. **The Choreogra-
        phic Art.** New York: Knopf, 1963.
        GV 1782.V3 1963

        This good treatise on choreography contains some
        material on Adam's ballets, including a scenario for
        Giselle (pages 287-297), part of a camera script for a
        movie **Giselle** (pages 336-337), and a brief history of
        La fille du Danube on page 354. Another edition was
        published in 1963 by Black, London.

71.   Willis, John. **Dance World.** New York: Crown, 1966-
        79.
        GV 1580.D335   ISSN 0070-2692

        Annual on the dance, with miscellaneous data on
        Adam's ballets.

72.   Wilson, George Buckley Laird. **A Dictionary of Ballet.**
        3d ed. New York: Theatre Arts Books, 1974.
        GV 1585.W5 1974   ISBN 0878300392

        General reference book on the ballet with some
        material on Adam and his ballets. Other editions were
        published in 1961 by Cassell, London, and in 1975 by
        Penguin Books, Harmondsworth.

INDIVIDUAL BALLETS

FAUST

73. "Theatricals." **Figaro in London** (March 9, 1833):
     39–40.

     On the first production of **Faust.**

LA FILLE DU DANUBE

74. Aschengreen, Erik. "The Beautiful Danger: Facets of
     the Romantic Ballet." **Dance Perspectives** 58
     (Summer 1974): 17–18. Citation also used
     following item 82.

     This portion of an issue entirely devoted to the
     romantic ballet is a very good history and analysis
     of **La fille du Danube.**

75. Beaumont, Cyril W. **Complete Book of Ballets: A Guide
     to the Principal Ballets of the Nineteenth and
     Twentieth Centuries.** London: Putnam, 1937,
     pp. 120–25. Citation also used following items 94,
     251, 266, 275, 279, 284, and 293.
     GV 1787.B35

     History and plot. In addition to item 76 below,
     other editions were published in 1938 by Putnam,
     New York, and in 1956 by Putnam, London.

76. ———— . **Complete Book of Ballets: A Guide to the
     Principal Ballets of the Nineteenth and Twentieth
     Centuries.** Garden City, N.Y.: Garden City
     Publishing Co., 1941, pp. 99–103. Citation also
     used following items 94, 251, 266, 275, 279, 284,
     and 293.
     MT 95.B4 1941

     History and plot.

77. Déaddé, Édouard. **La fille du Danube, ou, Ne m'oubliez
     pas.** Brussels: A. Jouhard, 1836.

     Play based on **La fille du Danube.**

78. Guest, Ivor. **Victorian Ballet–Girl: The Tragic Story
     of Clara Webster.** London: Black, 1957, pp. 46–49.
     Citation also used following item 253.
     GV 1785.W4 G8

On the performance of **La fille du Danube** by the ballerina.

79.   **The Simon and Schuster Book of the Ballet: A Complete Reference Guide, 1581 to the Present.** New York: Simon and Schuster, 1980, pp. 101–02. Citation also used following items 154, 254, 270 and preceding item 287.
      GV 1787.B275313   ISBN 067411223X

      History and plot; translation of **Il balletto: Repertorio del teatro di danza dal 1581.**

80.   Taglioni, Fillippo. **La fille du Danube: Ballet pantomime en deux actes et en quatre tableaux.** Paris: D. Jonas, 1836.

      Scenario; two versions published, with and without music.

GISELLE

1. History, plots, other general works

(The history and plot materials below, which vary in content, were selected from a wide body of literature)

81.   **Almanach des Königl. Hof. und National-Theaters des Königl. Residenz Theaters zu München für das Jahr 1892.** Munich: Bruckmann'sche Buchdruckerei, 1893.

      Yearbook containing some material on the performance of **Giselle** in Munich.

82.   Anderson, Jack. "Giselle: A Ballet in Two Acts." **Dance Magazine** 42 (December 1968): 45–68.

      Pages 45–51 are a very good history of **Giselle** and its performance, with illustrations of historical interest. Pages 52–67 contain the story of the ballet, with many photos, as staged by the American Ballet Theatre in 1968. Overall, this is one of the best articles on **Giselle.**

*   Aschengreen, Erik. "The Beautiful Danger," pp. 25–32. Cited above as item 74.

      Very good history and analysis of **Giselle** and Théophile Gautier's relationship to the ballet, putting the ballet in the historical context of French romanticism. This is one of the best articles on **Giselle.**

83.   Ashton, Geoffrey. **Giselle.** Woodbury, N.Y.:
          Barron's, 1985.
       GV 1790.G5 A74 1985   ISBN 0812056736

          Story of the ballet.

84.   Audsley, James. **The Book of Ballet.** 3d rev. ed.
          London: F. Warne, 1967, pp. 39–41.
       GV 1787.A8 1967   ISBN 0723203695

          Very good material on the nature of the leading
       dancing parts of **Giselle,** and also a description of
       two unusual presentations of the ballet in 1966
       (Bremen, Germany and Cuba).

85.   Austin, Richard. **Images of the Dance.** London: Vision
          Press, 1975
       GV 1787.A86   ISBN 0854782931

          This general history and criticism of ballet has
       some good information on the history of **Giselle,**
       particularly pages 103–10.

86.   Bakhrushin, ĪŪrii Alekseevich. **Istoriīa russkogo
          baleta.** 2nd ed. Moscow: Prosveshchenie, 1973,
          pp. 106–26.
       GV 1787.B22 1973

          Contains some material on the history of **Giselle** in
       Russia.

87.   Balanchine, George. **Balanchine's Complete Stories of
          the Great Ballets.** Edited by Francis Mason.
          Garden City, N.Y.: Doubleday, 1954, pp. 168–88.
       MT 95.B3

          History and plot.

88.   ———— . **Balanchine's New Complete Stories of the
          Great Ballets.** Edited by Francis Mason. Garden
          City, N.Y.: Doubleday, 1968, pp. 179–87. Citation
          also used following item 284.
       MT 95.B3 1968

          History and plot.

89.   Balanchine, George, and Francis Mason. **Balanchine's
          Complete Stories of the Great Ballets.** Rev. and
          enlarged ed. Garden City, N.Y.: Doubleday, 1977,
          pp. 262–74. Citation also used following items 284
          and 297.

MT 95.B3 1977   ISBN 0385113811

  History and plot.

90. _____ . **101 Stories of Great Ballets.** Garden
     City, N.Y.: Dolphin Books, 1975, pp. 193–209.
     Citation also used following 297.
     MT 95.B3 1975   ISBN 0385033982

  History and plot

91. Beaumont, Cyril W. **The Ballet Called Giselle.**
     London: C.W. Beaumont, 1944. 140 p.
     GV 1790.G5 B4 1944

  Best English–language work on **Giselle.** This comprehensive classic covers the history of the ballet,
Adam's music, the production of the ballet, and other
aspects. The book has some valuable illustrations.

92. _____ . **The Ballet Called Giselle.** London: C.W.
     Beaumont, 1945. 141 p.
     GV 1790.G5 B4 1945

  Revised edition of item 91.

93. _____ . **The Ballet Called Giselle.** Brooklyn: Dance
     Horizons, 1969. 141 p.
     GV 1790.G5 B4 1969

  Reprint of item 92.

94. _____ . **Ballet Design, Past and Present.** London:
     Studio, 1946. Citation also used following item
     284.
     GV 1787.B33

  This well–illustrated treatise on ballet sets and
costumes includes material on **Giselle.**

*   _____ . **Complete Book of Ballets,** pp. 156–67.
     Cited above as item 75.

  History and plot.

*   _____ . **Complete Book of Ballets,** pp. 129–37.
     Cited above as item 76.

  History and plot.

95. _____ . **Dancers Under My Lens: Essays in Ballet
     Criticism.** London: C.W. Beaumont, 1949,

pp. 80-87, 156-60.

History and criticism of **Giselle.**

96.   Bellew, Hélène. **Ballet in Moscow Today.** London:
      Thames and Hudson, 1956.

      Has some information on **Giselle** as performed in
      the Soviet Union. Another edition was published in
      1956 by the New York Graphic Society.

97.   Benois, Alexander. **Reminiscences of the Russian
      Ballet.** London: Putnam, 1941, pp. 69-72.
      GV 1787.B49

      On Giselle as performed in Russia. The memoirs
      cover the late 19th and early 20th centuries.

98.   Binney, Edwin. **Les ballets de Théophile Gautier.**
      Paris: Nizet, 1965, pp. 81-104, 335-50.
      PQ 2258.Z5 B5

      Pages 81-104 are on the sources for **Giselle** and
      Gautier's contributions to the ballet. The author con-
      tends that the ideas for the plot may be due more to
      Gautier than to Heinrich Heine, who is normally con-
      sidered to be the source of the ballet's concept. The
      revival of the ballet in 1863 is covered in detail on
      pages 335-350. The book has a number of good plates,
      including portraits of Adam, Gautier, Coralli, Saint-
      Georges and Perrot. This is one of the better
      publications on **Giselle.**

99.   Bol'shoĭ Teatr SSSR. Balet. **Zhizel': Balet v dvukh
      deĭstviiakh.** Moscow: Bol'shoĭ Teatr, 1968.

      Eleven page history and synopsis of the ballet as
      presented at the Bolshoi.

100. _____ . **Zhizel': Balet v dvukh deĭstviiakh.** Moscow:
      Bol'shoi Teatr, 1975.

      Seven page history and synopsis of the ballet, as
      presented at the Bolshoi.

101. Brinson, Peter. **Background to European Ballet: A
      Notebook from Its Archives.** Leyden: Sijthoff,
      1966, pp. 39-41.
      GV 1787.B66

      On the production of **Giselle** in Italy in the 1840's

and 1850's.

102. Brinson, Peter, and Clement Crisp. **The International
      Book of Ballet.** New York: Stein and Day, 1971,
      pp. 29–34.
      MT 95.B79 1971.   ISBN 0812813316

      History and plot. A 1970 London edition was
      published under the title **Ballet for All.**

103. Brown, Estelle T. "Romanticism as Manifested in
      Ballet." **Ball State University Forum** 15 (Summer
      1974): 39–45.

      Includes material about **Giselle** as a prime example
      of romanticism in ballet.

104. Buckle, Richard. **Modern Ballet Design: A Picture
      Book with Notes.** New York: Macmillan, 1955,
      pp. 2–3, 22, 33, 42–44.

      On ballet scenery and costume for **Giselle,** with
      good illustrations. Another edition was published in
      1955 by Black, London.

105. _____ . "Monsters at Midnight: The French Romantic
      Movement in Literature as a Background to the
      Ballet, 'Giselle'." **Dance and Dancers** 17 (April
      1966): 36–38; (May 1966): 22–27; (June 1966):
      22–27.

      Discusses French romantic literature and its
      relationship to and influence on **Giselle.**

106. Clarke, Mary, and Clement Crisp. **The Ballet Goer's
      Guide.** New York: Knopf, 1981, pp. 137–40.
      Citation also used preceding item 285.
      GV 1787.C563 1981   ISBN 039451307X

      History and plot.

107. Crosland, Margaret. **Ballet Carnival: A Companion to
      Ballet.** London: Arco, 1957, pp. 212–17.

      History and plot. Another edition was published
      in 1955.

108. Crowle, Pigeon. **Tales from the Ballet.** London:
      Faber & Faber, 1953, pp. 100–15.
      MT 95.C8 1953

History and plot. Another edition was published in
1953 by Pitman, New York.

109.   Davidson, Gladys. **Stories of the Ballets.** London:
       W. Laurie, 1958, pp. 77–89, 473–74.

       Pages 77–89 give the plot of **Giselle** and pages
       473–474 give some historical data and a list of
       productions. Another edition was published by Laurie
       in 1949.

110.   Davis, Jesse. **Classics of the Royal Ballet.**
       New York: Coward, McCann & Geoghegan, 1980,
       pp. 52–61.

       Well-illustrated story of the ballet as performed
       by the Royal Ballet, written for juveniles.

111.   Detaille, Georges, and Gérard Mulys. **Les ballets de
       Monte-Carlo, 1911–1944.** Paris: Editions Arc-en-
       ciel, 1954, pp. 18–19.

       History and plot of **Giselle** as performed in Monte
       Carlo.

112.   Drew, David, ed. **The Decca Book of Ballet.** London:
       F. Muller, 1958, pp. 25–32.
       MT 95.D74

       History, plot and musical themes.

113.   Ewen, David. **The Complete Book of Classical Music.**
       Englewood Cliffs, N.J.: Prentice-Hall, 1965,
       pp. 416–17. Citation also used following items
       330 and 383.

       Brief but significant reference article on **Giselle.**
       Ewen calls **Giselle's** score "remarkable," and quotes
       Théophile Gautier, "Adam's music is superior to the
       usual run of ballet music; it abounds in tunes and
       orchestral effects; it even includes a touching atten-
       tion for lovers of difficult music, a very well
       produced fugue." A short general essay on Adam is on
       pages 414–415.

114.   Gadan-Pamard, Francis, and Robert Maillard, eds.
       Dictionary of Modern Ballet. Translated from the
       French by John Montague and Peggie Cochrane.
       New York: Tudor Publishing Co., 1959, pp. 158–61.
       GV 1787.D513

Very good reference article (translation of item 115). The music of **Giselle** is called "simple and tuneful" and "theatrically right even though it could not withstand transference to the concert hall." Another English edition was published in 1959 by Methuen, London.

115.   _____ . **Dictionaire du ballet moderne.** Paris:
        F. Hazan, 1957.
        GV 1787.D5

Has a very good article on **Giselle.** Item 114 is the English translation.

116. Gautier, Théophile. **The Romantic Ballet as Seen by Théophile Gautier.** Translated from the French by Cyril W. Beaumont. London: C.W. Beaumont, 1932. Citation also used following item 252.

Fine book on the French romantic ballet, 1837-1848, including much on **Giselle.** Includes a section on Heinrich Heine's writings about the Wilis, which are considered to have been the inspiration for Gautier's development of the ballet. A reprint of this edition was published in 1980 by Books for Libraries, New York.
GV 1787.G35

117.   _____ . **The Romantic Ballet as Seen by Théophile Gautier.** Translated from the French by Cyril W. Beaumont. London: C.W. Beaumont, 1947. Citation also used following item 252.

Revision of item 116. A reprint of this edition was published in 1973 by Dance Horizons, Brooklyn.

118.   _____ . **Théâtre: Mystère, comédies et ballets.** Paris: Charpentier, 1872.

Has much material on 19th century French ballets, including a scenario of **Giselle.**

119. Gautier, Théophile, Jules Janin, and Philarète Chasles. **Les beautés de l'Opéra, ou, Chefs-d'oeuvre lyriques.** Paris: Soulié, 1845. MT 95.G27

This has a section on **Giselle,** and is valuable because it was published a few years after **Giselle's** premiere.

120. Gérard de Nerval, Gérard Labrunie, known as. **Notes
      d'un amateur de musique.** Paris: Les Cahiers de
      Paris, 1926.

      Book by a contemporary of Adam, with a section on
      Giselle.

121. **Giselle.** L'Avant-scène ballet/danse, vol. 1. Paris:
      L'Avant-scène, 1980.   178 p.
      GV 1580.A9 vol. 1.

      This French language collection of essays is the
      best source of information on **Giselle.** Included are:
      history and background of the ballet; detailed plot;
      detailed choreographic commentary; detailed analysis
      of the music; impressions of several ballerinas;
      commentary on performance; discography; outstanding
      bibliography; and many illustrations.

122. Goode, Gerald, ed. **The Book of Ballets, Classic and
      Modern.** New York: Crown, 1939, pp. 119-22.
      MT 95.G7

      History and plot, with two musical themes.

123. Goodwin, Noël. "Adam: Giselle: Comparative Table."
      Dance and Dancers 22 (June 1971): 32-33.

      Interesting table comparing the contents of four
      1961-1971 productions and a Decca recording. On the
      following pages (34-38), Goodwin, Peter Williams, and
      John Percival present three views of Mary Skeaping's
      production of **Giselle.**

124. ———— . "The Romantic North: Northern Ballet
      Theatre's New Production of Giselle." **Dance and
      Dancers** 30 (February 1979): 30-32.

      Good article on the performance of **Giselle** in
      England. The author gives an unusual description of
      Adam's music, stating that **Giselle** "may not be the
      most rewarding of ballet music for the orchestral
      player, but it does belong to that category of
      music. . .that the better it is played, the better it
      sounds."

125. Gruen, John. **The World's Great Ballets: La fille mal
      gardée to Davidsbündlertänze.** New York: Abrams,
      1981, pp. 28-30.
      GV 1790.A1   G78   ISBN 0810907259

History and plot.

126. Hall, George. **The Story of the Ballet: Giselle.**
      London: Ballet Books, 1961.

      Twenty-four page story of **Giselle.**

127. Haskell, Arnold L. **Ballet Panorama: An Illustrated
      Chronicle of Three Centuries.** 3d ed., rev. London:
      Batsford, 1948, pp. 48-50.

      On the history of **Giselle.** Also published were
      1938 and 1943 editions.

128. ———— . **Ballet Retrospect.** New York: Viking, 1965.
      GV 1785.H262 1965

      This general history and criticism of ballet has a
      moderate amount on **Giselle,** especially pages 49-51 and
      120-127.

129. Heath, Charles. **Beauties of the Opera and Ballet.**
      London: D. Bogue, 1845, pp. 1-16.

      History and plot, written just a few years after
      Giselle's premiere. A reprint was published in
      1977 by Da Capo, New York.

130. Jackson, Sheila. **Ballet in England: A Book of
      Lithographs.** London: Transatlantic Arts, 1945.

      Mostly illustrations of individual ballets, with
      some text; includes some material on **Giselle.**

131. Kerensky, Oleg. **Ballet Scene.** London:
      H. Hamilton, 1970, pp. 5-9.
      GV 1787.K37   1970   ISBN 0241018773

      Good general information on **Giselle.** This is
      identical to item 133.

132. ———— . **The Guinness Guide to Ballet.** Enfield,
      Middlesex: Guinness Superlatives Ltd., 1981,
      pp. 161-64.
      GV 1787.K36   ISBN 0851122264

      History, analysis, and plot.

133. ———— . **The World of Ballet.** New York: Coward-
      McCann, 1970, pp. 6-10.
      GV 1787.K37   1970b

Good general information on **Giselle.** This is
identical to item 131.

134. Kirstein, Lincoln. **Movement & Metaphor: Four
Centuries of Ballet.** New York: Praeger, 1970,
pp. 150–53.
GV 1787.K513

Well-written section on the history of **Giselle.**

135. Krokover, Rosalyn. **The New Borzoi Book of Ballets.**
New York: Knopf, 1956, pp. 133–42.
MT 95.K76

History and plot.

136. Lawrence, Robert. **The Victor Book of Ballets and
Ballet Music.** New York: Simon & Schuster, 1950,
pp. 210–20.
MT 95.L48

History and plot, with several musical themes.

137. Lifar, Serge. **Giselle: Apothéose du ballet romantique.** Paris: A. Michel, 1942. 300 p.
GV 1790.G5 L5

Substantial book on the history and criticism of
Giselle. The author is not favorable to Adam's music.
Thirteen years later, in his **La musique par la danse**
(item 56), he presented a much higher opinion of Adam.
A reprint was published in 1982.

138. Lopukhov, Fedor. **Khoreograficheskie otkrovennosti.**
Moscow: Iskusstvo, 1971.

This general treatise on ballet has a moderate
amount on **Giselle,** particularly pages 36–39.

139. Mannoni, Gérard. **Grands ballets de l'Opéra de Paris.**
Paris: Sylvie Messinger et Théâtre national de
l'Opéra de Paris, 1982, pp. 32–55.

Well-illustrated, excellent comprehensive essay on
Giselle; one of the best sources, taking into account
the combination of quality, quantity, and scope.

140. Martin, John Joseph. "Reports from Russia." **Dance
Magazine** 30 (September 1956): 14–21, 58–64.
Citation also used following item 286.

Has some material on the Russian production of

Giselle.

141. Moore, Lillian. "Like Cinderella, Giselle Once Went
     to a Ball." **Dance News** 24 (April 1954): 7-8.

     Using a three-act 1844 Italian version of **Giselle**
     as a prime example, demonstrates that early versions
     of **Giselle** varied considerably and that any claims
     of authenticity of any particular early version are
     questionable.

142. Morley, Iris. **Soviet Ballet.** London: Collins, 1945,
     pp. 34-37.
     GV 1787.M6

     On **Giselle** as performed in the Soviet Union.

143. Nahum, Stirling Henry, and Arnold L. Haskell. **Baron
     at the Ballet.** New York: Morrow, 1951, pp. 25-40.

     History and criticism of **Giselle,** predominantly
     photos (by Nahum) with some text (by Haskell).
     Another edition was published in 1950 by Collins,
     London.

144. ———. **Baron Encore.** London: Collins, 1952,
     pp. 17-22.
     GV 1787.N32

     Short section on **Giselle,** mostly photos (by Nahum)
     with some text (by Haskell), featuring the dancing of
     Yvette Chauviré.

145. Niehaus, Max. **Himmel, Hölle und Trikot: Heinrich
     Heine und das Ballet.** Munich: Nymphenburger
     Verlagshandlung, 1959.
     GV 1787.N5

     On Heine's relationship and contributions to
     ballet. His book, **De l'Allemagne,** gave Théophile
     Gautier the idea for **Giselle.**

146. Posner, Sandy. **Giselle: The Story of the Ballet.**
     London: Newman Wolsey, 1946.

     Illustrated story of the ballet. At least four
     other editions were published.

147. Rebling, Eberhard. **Ballett von A bis Z.** Berlin:
     Henschel, 1966, pp. 147-52. Citation also used
     following item 286.

MT 95.R33

Plot and discussion of **Giselle.**

148. Regner, Otto Friedrich, ed. **Reclams Balletführer.**
     Stuttgart: Reclam-Verlag, 1956, pp. 145-54.

     History and plot. At least five editions were
     published.

149. Reynolds, Nancy, and Susan Reimer-Torn.
     **In Performance: A Companion to the Classics of the
     Dance.** New York: Harmony Books, 1980, pp. 7-12.
     Citation also used preceding item 287.
     GV 1781.R44 1980   ISBN 0517539926

     History and plot.

150. Ries, Frank W.D. "In Search of Giselle: 'Travels
     with a Chameleon Romantic'." **Dance Magazine** 53
     (August 1979): 59-74.

     History of changes of production of **Giselle.**

151. Robert, Grace. **The Borzoi Book of Ballets.**
     New York: Knopf, 1946, pp. 156-80.
     GV 1787.R6

     History and plot.

152. Roseveare, Ursula. **Selected Stories from the Ballet.**
     London: Pitman, 1954, pp. 85-95.
     MT 95.R76

     History and plot for a juvenile audience.

153. Severn, Merlyn, and Arnold L. Haskell. **Ballet in
     Action.** London: J. Lane, 1938, pp. 16-19, 118.

     Material on performance of **Giselle,** mostly photos,
     (by Severn) with some text (by Haskell).

154. Seymour, Maurice. **Seymour on Ballet: 101 Photographs.**
     Chicago: Pellegrini and Cudahy, 1947, plates 1-4.
     GV 787.S34

     Four plates of photos on performance of **Giselle,**
     with brief explanatory text.

*   The Simon and Schuster Book of the Ballet, pp. 105-08.
       Cited above as item 79.

       History and plot.

155.   Slonimskiĭ, I͡Uriĭ Iosifovich. **Zhizel'**. Leningrad:
       Izd. Len. gos. teatra opery i baleta, 1934.

       Twenty-one page synopsis.

156.   ———— . **Zhizel': Eti͡udy.** Leningrad: Muzyka, 1969.

       General work on **Giselle.**

157.   ———— . **Zhizel' balet.** Leningrad: Academia, 1976.

       General work on **Giselle.**

158.   **100 [Sto] baletnykh libretto.** Moscow: Muzyka, 1966,
       pp. 21-25. Citation also used following item 287.
       ML 48.S72

       History and plot.

159.   Terry, Walter. **Ballet: A New Guide to the Liveliest
       Art.** New York: Dell, 1959, pp. 152-58.
       GV 1787.T32

       Well-written history and plot.

160.   ———— . **Ballet Guide: Background, Listings, Credits,
       and Descriptions of More Than Five Hundred of the
       World's Major Ballets.** New York: Dodd, Mead,
       1976, pp. 160-66. Citation also used following
       items 270 and 287.
       GV 1790.A1 T47   ISBN 0396070248

       History and plot.

161.   Testa, Alberto, ed. **Giselle.** La danza e il balletto,
       no. 1. Rome: Di Giacomo, 1980. 119 p.
       GV 1790.G5 G58 1980

       General book on **Giselle,** in Italian.

162.   Untermeyer, Louis. **Tales from the Ballet.** New York:
       Golden Press, 1968, pp. 61-66.
       ML 3930.A2 U5

       Illustrated juvenile story of **Giselle.**

163. Vaillat, Léandre. **Ballets de l'Opéra de Paris.**
     Paris: Compagnie française des arts graphiques,
     1943.

     This book on the ballets performed by the Paris
     Opéra contains some material on **Giselle.**

164. Verdy, Violette. **Giselle, A Role for a Lifetime.**
     New York: M. Dekker, 1977. 80 p.
     GV 1790.G5 V47   ISBN 0824765257

     Pleasant monograph by a former ballerina. Included
     is a text of the ballet scenario and a section on her
     impressions of dancing the ballet.

165. _____. **Giselle, or The Wilis.** Adapted from
     Théophile Gautier. New York: McGraw-Hill, 1970.
     50 p.
     ML 3930.A3 V5

     Illustrated story of the ballet.

166. Verwer, Hans. **Guide to the Ballet.** Translated from
     the Dutch by Henry Mins. New York: Barnes and
     Noble, 1963, pp. 28-35.
     GV 1787.V383

     History and plot.

167. Viveash, Cherry. **Tales from the Ballet.** London:
     G. Ronald, 1958, pp. 43-49.

     History and plot.

168. Waldman, Max. **Waldman on Dance.** New York: Morrow,
     1977.
     GV 1785.A1 W26   ISBN 0688032273

     Has photos of three productions of **Giselle,** with a
     little text.

169. Winkler, H.J. **Oper und Ballett.** Munich: Südwest
     Verlag, 1964, pp. 365-66. Citation also used
     following items 355 and 388.

     History and plot.

170. Wolff, Stéphane. **L'Opéra au Palais Garnier, 1875–
     1962: Les oeuvres, les interprètes.** Paris:
     L'Entr'acte, 1962, pp. 282-83.
     ML 1727.8.P2 W8

Valuable basic data on **Giselle** as performed at
the Palais Garnier.

2.   Scenarios

171. Ronzani, Domenico. **Gisella, o, Le Villi.** Rome: Tip.
      Puccinelli, [1845?].

172. Saint-Georges, Jules Henri Vernoy de, and Théophile
      Gautier. **Gisella: Ballo fantastico in tre atti.**
      Naples: Tip. Flautina, 1849.

173. ———— . **Gisella: Ballo in tre atti.** Naples: 1849.

174. ———— . **Gisella, o, Le Wili: Baletto fantastico.**
      Bologna: Tip. delle bele arti, 1843.

175. ———— . **Gisella, o, Le Wili: Ballo fantastico in due
      atti.** Turin: Tip. teatrale di Savoiardo, 1866.

176. ———— . **Gisella, oder, Die Wilis: Phantastisches
      Ballet in zwey Aufzügen.** Vienna: F. Ullrich,
      [ca. 1850].

177. ———— . **Gisella, ossia, Il ballo notturno.**
      Florence: Tip. Galletti, 1845.

178. ———— . **Giselle, ou, Les Wilis: Ballet fantastique
      en deux actes.** Paris: Ve. Jonas, 1841.

179. ———— . **Giselle, ou, Les Wilis: Ballet fantastique
      en deux actes.** Paris: M. Lévy, 1845.

180. ———— . **Giselle, ou, Les Wilis: Ballet fantastique
      en deux actes.** Paris-Versailles: H. Le Boulch,
      [1924?].

181. ———— . **Giselle, ou, Les Wilis: Ballet pantomime
      en deux actes.** Paris: Typ. Lacrampe, [186-?].

182. ———— . **Giselle: Romantisk ballet in 2 akter.**
      Copenhagen: J.H. Schubothes, 1862.

183. ———— . **Zhizel', ili, Vilisi.** Saint Petersburg,
      1889.

      Probable title. The item was not seen nor veri-
fied. It was cited in a bibliography as **Jizel ili
vilisi.**

3. Characters

184. Fehl, Fred, and Doris Hering. **Giselle & Albrecht.**
     New York: Dance Horizons, 1981. 191 p.
     GV 1790.G5 F43 1981   ISBN 0871271249

     Very well done monograph on the roles of Giselle
     and Albrecht, consisting of Hering's background his-
     torical essays and Fehl's many photos of several
     dancers in the two roles.

185. Mueller, John. "Is Giselle a Virgin?"
     Dance Chronicle 4, no. 2 (1981): 151-54.

     Most interesting essay explaining why Giselle
     suddenly descends into madness on discovering she has
     been deceived by Albrecht. The author rejects
     Cyril Beaumont's contention that Giselle was very
     neurotic, and instead proposes that Giselle and
     Albrecht had been lovers, and Giselle felt jilted and
     dishonored by the deception.

186. Terry, Walter. "What Is Albrecht to 'Giselle'?"
     Saturday Review 51 (May 4, 1968): 44-45.

     Fine essay on the Albrecht role.

4. Music

187. Dorris, George. "The Music of Giselle." **Ballet
     Review** 4 (Summer 1972): 61-67.

     Extended commentary on two 1971 recordings of the
     complete **Giselle.** In addition, it is a very good
     overall analysis of the ballet's music.

188. Fiske, Roger. **Ballet Music.** London: G. Harrap,
     1958, pp. 14-21.
     MT 95.F5

     Excellent commentary on the music of **Giselle,**
     with 18 musical themes given. It is perhaps the best
     treatment of the ballet's music.

189. Searle, Humphrey. **Ballet Music: An Introduction.**
     London: Cassell, 1958, pp. 56-59.
     ML 3460.S4

     Well-written, thoughtful essay on the music of
     Giselle, generally favorable to Adam. Another edition
     was published in 1973.

190. _____ . "The Grand Romantic Ballets." **Perspectives in Music.** Edited by Leroy Ostransky. Englewood Cliffs, N.J.: Prentice-Hall, 1963, pp. 265-67.
ML 90.075

Same basic essay as item 189.

5. Choreography

191. **Choreography by George Balanchine: A Catalogue of Works.** New York: Viking, 1984, pp. 173-74.

On Balanchine's choreography for **Giselle.** `Another edition was published in 1983 by Eakins Press Foundation, New York.

192. Flury, Philip, and Peter Kaufmann. **Heinz Spoerli Ballett-Faszination.** Zürich: Fretz Verlag, 1983, pp. 40, 69-73.
GV 1785.S7 F58 1983   ISBN 385692003X

On the choreography of **Giselle** and **Giselle pas de deux,** as done by Spoerli.

193. Sergeev, Konstantin Mikhailovich. **Giselle: Excerpts.** New York: Dance Notation Bureau, 1957-66.

Dance notation for **Giselle** by various persons.

194. Vaughan, David. **Frederick Ashton and His Ballets.** London: Black, 1977.
GV 1785.A8 V38 1977b   ISBN 071361689X

Has some material on the choreography for **Giselle** as done by Ashton. Another edition was published in 1977 by Knopf, New York.

6. Dancers and dance companies in relation to **Giselle**

(The following is a selective sample. Many works on dancers and dance companies contain relevant material)

195. Alonso, Alicia. "Performing Giselle." **American Ballet Theatre.** Text and commentary by Charles Payne. New York: Knopf, 1978, pp. 333-42.
GV 1786.A43 A44   ISBN 0394498356

On her performance in **Giselle** for the American Ballet Theatre.

196. Alovert, Nina. **Baryshnikov in Russia.** Translated by Irene Huntoon. New York: Holt, Rinehart and Winston, 1984, pp. 91-129.

GV 1785.B348   A76   1984   ISBN 0030625890

On Baryshnikov's performance in **Giselle** while in
Russia, with many photos.

197.   Anthony, Gordon. **Studies of Dancers in Colour and
       Monochrome.** London: Home & Van Thal, 1948,
       pp. 9 and 11, and plates 17–18.
       GV 1785.A1   A63

       Two photographs of Robert Helpman as Albrecht, plus
some text.

198.   Austin, Richard. **The Ballerina.** London: Vision
       Press, 1974.
       GV 1787.A85

       Treatise on ballerinas, with biographical sketches,
containing some good material on the performance of
Giselle, particularly pages 35–38 and 47–54.

199.   _____ . **Natalia Makarova, Ballerina.** Brooklyn, N.Y.:
       Dance Horizons, 1978.
       GV 185.M26   A96   ISBN 0871271036

       Biography of the ballerina, with material on her
performance in **Giselle.** Another edition was published
by Dance Books, London.

200.   Bland, Alexander. **The Nureyev Image.** London: udio
       Studio Vista, 1976. Citation also used preceding
       item 292.
       GV 1785.N8   B57   ISBN 028970362X

       Photo-biography of the dancer, including material
on his performance in **Giselle.** Another edition was
published in 1976 by Quadrangle, New York.

201.   **The Bolshoi Ballet: Ballet Company of the Bolshoi
       Theatre of the U.S.S.R.** Moscow: Planeta, 1981,
       pp. 68–79.
       GV 1786.B64   B64   1981

       On **Giselle** as performed by the Bolshoi over the
years, with many illustrations.

202.   **The Bolshoi Ballet Story.** New York: Heller & Heller,
       1959, pp. 104–05.
       GV 1786.M6   B6

       On **Giselle** as performed by the Bolshoi.

203. Bruhn, Erik. "Restaging the Classics." **American Ballet Theatre.** Text and commentary by Charles Payne. New York: Knopf, 1978, pp. 317–32.

GV 1786.A43 A44   ISBN 0394498356

Primarily on **Giselle** as performed by the American Ballet Theatre.

204. Cameron, Judy, and Walter Terry. **The Bolshoi Ballet.** New York: Harper & Row, 1975, pp. 20–23.
GV 1786.M6 C35   ISBN 0064306003

Section of performance photos of **Giselle** by the Bolshoi (taken by Cameron), with brief notes by Terry.

205. Clarke, Mary. **The Sadler's Wells Ballet: A History and an Appreciation.** London: Black, 1955.
GV 1786.S3 C6

History of the company, with some material on **Giselle.** Another edition was published in 1955 by Macmillan, New York.

206. Crowle, Pigeon. **Moira Shearer: Portrait of a Dancer.** London: Faber & Faber, 1951.

Includes text and photos on the ballerina's performance in **Giselle.** Another edition was published by Faber & Faber in 1949 and by Pitman, New York, in 1951.

207. Dolin, Anton. **Markova, Her Life and Art.** London: W.H. Allen, 1953.

Biography of the ballerina, with material on her performance in **Giselle.** Another edition was published in 1973 by White Lion, London.

208. ———— . **The Sleeping Ballerina.** London: F. Muller, 1966.
GV 1785.S67 D6

Biography of the ballerina Olga Spessivtzeva, with a moderate amount on her performance in **Giselle.**

209. Fisher, Hugh, ed. **Festival Ballet.** London: Black, 1953, pp. 7–9.

On the performance of **Giselle** by the Festival Ballet Company.

210. Fisher, Hugh. **The Sadler's Wells Theatre Ballet.**
     London: Black, 1956, p. 31.
     GV 1786.S3 F49

     On the company's performance of **Giselle pas de deux**
     during the 1946-1956 period. Another edition was pub-
     lished in 1956 by Pitman, New York.

211. Franks, Arthur Henry. **Pavlova: A Biography.** London:
     Burke, 1956.
     GV 1785.P3 F7

     Biography of the ballerina, with material on her
     performance of **Giselle.** Another edition was pub-
     lished in 1956 by Macmillan, New York.

212. _____ . **Svetlana Beriosova: A Biography.** London:
     Burke, 1958.
     GV 1785.B44 F7

     Biography of the ballerina, with material on her
     performance in **Giselle.**

213. Gamez, Tana de. **Alicia Alonso at Home and Abroad.**
     New York: Citadel Press, 1971.
     GV 1785.A63 D43   ISBN 0806502185

     Biography of the ballerina, with a moderate amount
     of material on her performance as **Giselle,**
     particularly pages 139-55.

214. Gillard, David. **Beryl Grey: A Biography.** London:
     W. H. Allen, 1977.
     GV 1785.G72 G54   ISBN 0491022212

     Biography of the ballerina with material on her
     performance in **Giselle.**

215. Gregory, John, and Alexander Ukladnikov. **Leningrad's**
     Ballet: Maryinsky to Kirov. London: Robson
     Books, 1981, pp. 124-27.
     GV 1786.L46 G73 1971   ISBN 0860511103

     On the performance of **Giselle** by the Kirov Ballet.
     Another edition was published in 1980 by Universe
     Books, New York.

216. Gruen, John. **Erik Bruhn, Danseur Noble.** New York:
     Viking Press, 1979.
     GV 1785.B78 G78   ISBN 0670297712

Biography of the dancer, with material on his performance in **Giselle.**

217. Guest, Ivor. **Fanny Cerrito: The Life of a Romantic Ballerina.** Charing Cross: Phoenix House, 1956. Citation also used preceding item 282.
GV 1785.C43 G8

Biography of the ballerina with some material on **Giselle.**

*   ———— . **Fanny Elssler.** Cited above as item 50.

Biography of the ballerina, with material on **Giselle.**

218. ———— . "The Two Giselles of the Romantic Ballet." **Dancing Times,** no. 699 (December 1968): 139–41.

Contrasts Carlotta Grisi and Fanny Elssler in the role of **Giselle,** and is supportive of the lesser known Elssler.

219. Hart, John. **The Royal Ballet in Performance at Covent Garden.** London: Faber & Faber, 1958.
GV 1786.R6 H3 1958

On the performance of the company with some material on **Giselle.** Another edition was published in 1959 by Coward-McCann, New York.

220. Huckenphaler, Victoria. **Ballerina: A Biography of Violette Verdy.** New York: Audience Arts, 1978.
GV 1785.V47 H83   ISBN 0824765184

Biography of the ballerina, with material on her performance in **Giselle.**

221. Ilyin, Eugene K. "Tragedy of a Living 'Giselle': The Story of Olga Spessivtzeva." **Dance Magazine** 28 (June 1954): 21–23, 54–55.

Tragic story of a ballerina whose performance in **Giselle** was outstanding.

222. Kerensky, Oleg. **Anna Pavlova.** New York: Dutton, 1973.
GV 1785.P3 K47 1973   ISBN 0525176586

Biography of the ballerina, with material on her performance in **Giselle.** Another edition was published in 1973 by Hamilton, London.

223. Kocho, Boris. **Diaghilev and the Ballets Russes.**
      Translated from the French by Adrienne Foulke.
      New York: Harper & Row, 1970, pp. 48-51.
      GV 1785.D5 K613 1970

      History of the company's performance of **Giselle.**

224. Lieven, Peter. **The Birth of Ballets-Russes.**
      Translated by L. Zarine. New York: Dover, 1973,
      pp. 110-13.

      History of the company's performance of **Giselle.**
      Another edition was published in 1936 by Allen & Unwin,
      London.

225. Lifar, Serge. **The Three Graces: Anna Pavlova, Tamara
      Karsavina, Olga Spessivtzeva: The Legends and the
      Truth.** London: Cassell, 1959.
      GV 1785.A1 L513

      Biographies of the three ballerinas, with some
      material on their performances in **Giselle.** This is a
      translation of **Les trois grâces du XXe siècle** (1959).

226. _____ . **Carlotta Grisi.** Paris: A. Michel, 1941.
      GV 1785.G73 L5

      Biography of the ballerina, with some material on
      her performance in **Giselle,** and on music used in
      Giselle other than that of Adam. This is somewhat
      different from the English edition (item 227).

227. _____ . **Carlotta Grisi.** Translated from the French
      with an introduction by Doris Langley Moore.
      London: J. Lehmann, 1947.
      GV 1785.G73 L52

      Translation of item 226, but somewhat different.

228. L'vov-Anokhin, Boris Aleksandrovich. **Galina Ulanova.**
      Moscow: Iskusstvo, 1970, pp. 53-76. Citation also
      used following item 294.

      On the performance of the ballerina in **Giselle.**

229. Macdonald, Nesta. "Two Giselles, Karsavina and Pav-
      lova: The Diaghilev Ballet's Second London Season.
      Dancing Times, no. 733 (October 1971): 19-22.

On the two ballerinas' performances in **Giselle** during 1911.

230. Makarova, Natalia. **A Dance Autobiography.** New York: Knopf, 1979.
GV 1785.M26 A35 1979   ISBN 0394501411

Autobiography of the ballerina, with some material on her performance in **Giselle.**

231. Markova, Alicia. **Giselle and I.** London: `Barrie and Rockcliff, 1960.
GV 1785.M3 A3

Very good monograph on Markova's performance in **Giselle,** and her commentary on the ballet.

232. ─────. **Giselle and I.** New York: Vanguard Press, 1961.
GV 1785.M3 A3 1961

Same as 1960 edition.

233. Martin, John Joseph. "Another Link in the History of Giselle." **Dance Magazine** 29 (July 1955): 14–21.

On Erik Bruhn and Alicia Markova performing **Giselle,** with Markova passing down the ballet's traditions.

234. Maynard, Olga. "Natalia Makarova, Giselle for Today." **Dance Magazine** 53 (August 1979): 75–79.

On the ballerina's performance in **Giselle.**

235. Money, Keith. **Fonteyn, the Making of a Legend.** London: Collins, 1973, pp. 42–49. Citation also used following item 293.
GV 1785.F63 M65   ISBN 0002112450

On the ballerina's performance in **Giselle.**

236. Moore, Lillian. "Mary Ann Lee, First American Giselle." **Chronicles of the American Dance.** Edited by Paul David Magriel. New York: Holt, 1948, pp. 102–17.

Biography of the ballerina who first performed **Giselle** in the United States. Reprinted in 1978 by Da Capo Press, New York.

237. **Segodnia na stsene Bol'shogo teatra, 1776–1976.**
      Moscow: Iskusstvo, 1976.

      History of the Bolshoi Ballet, including the
      performance of **Giselle.**

238. Smakov, Gennady. **Baryshnikov, From Russia to the
      West.** New York: Farrar Straus Giroux, 1981.
      Citation also used following item 293.
      GV 1785.B348 S6 1981   ISBN 0374109087

      Biography of the dancer, with material on his
      performance in **Giselle.**

239. Terry, Walter. **Alicia and Her Ballet nacional de
      Cuba: An Illustrated Biography of Alicia Alonso.**
      Garden City, N.Y.: Anchor Books, 1981.
      GV 1785.A63 T47   ISBN 0385149565

      Biography of the ballerina, with a fair amount of
      material on her performance in **Giselle.**

240. **Violetta Elvin.** Dancers of Today, no. 3. London:
      Black, 1953, pp. 12–13.

      On the ballerina's performance in **Giselle.**

                        7.   Movies

241. Braun, Susan, and Jessie Kitching, comps. **Dance and
      Mime Film and Videotape Catalog.** New York: Dance
      Films Association, 1980, pp. 2, 9, 38–39, 75, 84.
      Citation also used following item 293.
      GV 1594.D364 1980

      Annotations on movie versions of **Giselle.**

242. Mueller, John. **Dance Film Directory: An Annotated
      and Evaluative Guide to Films on Ballet and Modern
      Dance.** Princeton, N.J.: Princeton Book Co., 1979,
      pp. 20, 28–29, 41–42, 61. Citation also used
      following item 293.
      GV 1595.M89   ISBN 0916622088

      Evaluations of movie versions of **Giselle.**

243. _____ . "Films: The Ephemeral Giselle." **Dance
      Magazine** 48 (September 1974): 85.

      Listing and discussion of available films of the
      complete **Giselle.**

244. **Ten Years of Films on Ballet and Classical Dance,
     1956–1965: Catalogue.** Paris: UNESCO, 1968.
     GV 1790.A1 T4

     This annotated catalog of dance films, arranged
     by country, includes entries for **Giselle**.

8. Derivatives, adaptations etc.

(See also **Giselle's Revenge,** and
L'air d'esprit)

245. Daniels, Diana P. "Some Strange Giselles: Bizarre
     Adventures of a 19th Century Ballet." **Dance
     Magazine** 32 (July 1958): 52–55.

     History of various borrowings of the story of
     Giselle for theatrical purposes other than the
     original ballet.

246. Guest, Ivor. " 'Giselle' as an Opera and the Opera
     Burlesqued." **Ballet** 4 (October 1947): 13–18.

     On **Giselle** adapted into operatic form.

247. ————— . "Parodies of Giselle on the English Stage,
     1841–1871." **Theatre Notebook** 9 (January–March
     1955): 38–46.

     History of parodies of **Giselle** in England.

248. Loder, Edward James, and George Sloane. **The Night
     Dancers: A New Grand Romantic Opera in Three
     Parts, Partly Founded on the Story of Giselle.**
     2d ed. London: C. Jeffreys, 1846.

     Libretto of an opera partly based on **Giselle,** with
     music by Loder and story by Sloane.

249. Lorentz, Alcide Joseph. "Gris–aile balayette (petit
     balai) en deux actes de décès." **Musée, Philipon:
     Album de toute le monde.** Paris: Aubert, 1842,
     vol. 9, pp. 65–70.

     Parody of **Giselle**; cited only in item 59, year
     1975, vol. 1, p. 613.

250. Moncrieff, William Thomas. **Giselle, or, The Phantom
     Night Dancers.** London: J. Limbird, 1842.

     Play based on **Giselle.**

251. Sorley-Walker, Katherine. "Giselle as a Play."
         Ballet 2 (October 1946): 21-28.

      On **Giselle** adapted into an opera.

                    LA JOLIE FILLE DE GAND

         1.   History, plots, other general works.

*   Beaumont, Cyril W. **Complete Book of Ballets,**
         pp. 182-93. Cited above as item 75.

      History and plot.

*   _____ . **Complete Book of Ballets,** pp. 149-59.
         Cited above as item 76.

      History and plot.

252. Challamel, Augustin, ed. **Album de l'Opéra.** Paris: A.
         Challamel, 1844.

      Contains the plot of **La jolie fille de Gand.**

*   Gautier, Théophile. **The Romantic Ballet as Seen by**
         Théophile Gautier. Cited above as item 116.

      Fine book on the French romantic ballet, 1837-1848,
      including some material on **La jolie fille de Gand.**

*   _____ . **The Romantic Ballet as Seen by Théophile**
         Gautier. Cited above as item 117.

      Revision of previous item.

253. Guest, Ivor. "La jolie fille de Gand." **Dancing**
         Times, no. 671 (August 1966): 573-75.

      Historical background of the ballet.

*   _____ . **Victorian Ballet-girl,** pp. 90-92. Cited
         above as item 78.

      On the performance of **La jolie fille de Gand** by the
      ballerina Clara Webster.

254. Kerensky, Oleg. "Festival Ballet's Beatrix." **Dancing**
         Times, no. 673 (October 1966): 16-17.

      On the performance of **La jolie fille de Gand** by the
      Festival Ballet company.

*   **The Simon and Schuster Book of the Ballet,** pp. 111,

115. Cited above as item 79.

History and plot of **La jolie fille de Gand** and a variant, **Beatrice di Gand.**

2. Scenarios

255. Cortesi, Antonio. **La bella fanciulla di Gand.**
Bologna: Tip. Delle belle arti, 1852.

256. Saint-Georges, Jules Henri Vernoy de, and Albert
[François Decombe]. **Beatrice di Gand, ovvero, Un
sogno: Azione mimica in tre parti e nove quadri,**
Milan: Tip. G. Truffi, 1845.

257. _____ . **Beatrice di Gand, ovvero, Un sogno: Azione
mimica in tre parti e nove quadri.** Milan: Tip.
Valentini, 1847.

258. _____ . **Beatrice di Gand, ovvero, Un sogno: Azione
mimica in tre parti e nove quadri.** Verona: Tip.
di P. Bisesti, [1849?].

259. _____ . **La bella fanciulla di Gand: Ballo-
pantomime in tre parti.** Venice: G. Molinari,
1845-46.

260. _____ . **La bella fanciulla di Gand, ovvero, Un
sogno: Azione mimica in tre parti e nove quadri.**
Tip. Delle belle arti, 1852.

261. _____ . **La bella fanciulla di Gand, ovvero, Un sogno:
Azione mimica in otto quadri.** Turin: Tip. di C.
Fodratti, 1852.

262. _____ . **La jolie fille de Gand: Ballet pantomime en
trois actes et neuf tableau.** Paris: Ve. Jonas,
1845.

263. _____ . **The New Grand Ballet of the Beauty of Ghent:
As First Performed in this Country at the Theatre
Royal, Drury Lane, on Saturday, February 17th,
1844.** London: Nassau Steam Press, [1844?].

3. Derivatives, adaptations, etc.

264. Herz, Henri. **3 [Trois] airs de ballet de La jolie
fille de Gand: Arrangés en forme de divertissements pour le piano, op. 128.** London: Cramer,
Beale, [18--].

Three pieces adapted from **La jolie fille de Gand.**

265. ———— . **Trois divertissements pour le piano sur les airs de ballet: La jolie fille de Gand d'Ad. Adam, op. 128.** Mayence: B. Schott Fils, [18——].

Three pieces adapted from **La jolie fille de Gand.**

LE DIABLE À QUATRE

1. History, plots, other general works.

266. Barnes, Patricia. "Harkness à Quatre." **Dance and Dancers** 21 (April 1970): 38–39.

On the Harkness Ballet's production of **Le diable à quatre.**

*   Beaumont, Cyril W. **Complete Book of Ballets,** pp. 215–22. Cited above as item 75.

History and plot.

*   ———— . **Complete Book of Ballets,** pp. 177–83. Cited above as item 76.

History and plot.

267. "Le diable à quatre." **American Record Guide** 32 (March 1966): 591.

Commentary on a recording of the ballet.

268. Goldner, Nancy. "Harkness Ballet at Brooklyn Academy of Music, Nov. 6–18." **Dance News** 55 (December 1969): 10.

On the Harkness Ballet's production of **Le diable à quatre.**

269. Hering, Doris. "Three Years Later: A Review of the Netherlands Dance Theatre, New York City Center, April 9–21, 1968." **Dance Magazine** 42 (June 1968): 30, 32–33, 74–75.

On a production of a pas de deux from **Le diable à quatre.**

270. Schlivian, C. "Königliche Theater: Die Wieburkur und Carlotta Grisi." **Deutsche Theater–Zeitung** 4 (January 13, 1849): 115.

About Carlotta Grisi's performance in **Le diable à quatre.**

* **The Simon and Schuster Book of the Ballet,** p. 116. Cited above as item 79.

History and plot.

* Terry, Walter. **Ballet Guide,** p. 110. Cited above as item 160.

History and plot of the pas de deux from **Le diable à quatre.**

2. Scenarios

271. Casati, Giovanni. **Il diavolo a quattro: Azione coreografica in 4 parti.** Milan: Tip. di P.R. Carpano, 1855.

272. Leuven, Adolphe de, and Joseph Mazilier. **Le diable à quatre: A Fairy Ballet Pantomime in Two Acts and Five Tableaux.** New York: Sold by Mr. Corbyn's Dramatic Agency, 1848.

273. ———— . **Le diable à quatre: A Fairy Ballet Pantomime in 2 Acts and 5 Tableaux.** New York: M.L. Fiot, 1848.

274. ———— . **Le diable à quatre: Ballet pantomime en deux actes.** Paris: Mme. Ve. Jonas, 1845.

3. Derivatives, adaptations, etc.

(See also **Pas de Deux for Four**)

275. Rosellen, Henri. **Deux rondeaux pour le piano sur les motifs du ballet: "Diable à quatre" d'Ad. Adam, op. 77, nos. 1 & 2.** Boston: Wm. H. Oakes, [18—].

Two piano adaptations of music from **Le diable à quatre.**

THE MARBLE MAIDEN

* Beaumont, Cyril W. **Complete Book of Ballets,** pp. 394-96. Cited above as item 75.

History and plot.

* ———— . **Complete Book of Ballets,** pp. 323-24.

Cited above as item 76.

History and plot.

276. Saint-Georges, Jules Henri Vernoy de, and Albert
      [François Decombe]. **The Marble Maiden: As
      Performed for the First Time on Any Stage at the
      Theatre Royal, Drury Lane, on Saturday, September
      27th, 1845.** London: W.S. Johnson, [1845?].

      Scenario.

GRISELDIS

277. Dumanoir, Philippe François Pinel, and Joseph
      Mazilier. **Les Cinq Sens: Ballet pantomime en 3
      actes et 5 tableaux.** Paris: Impr. de Dondey-Dupré,
      1848.

      Scenario.

278. ———. **Griseldis, ou, Les cinq sens: Ballet
      pantomime en trois actes et cinq tableaux.** Paris:
      M. Lévy Frères, 1859.

      Scenario.

279. Guest, Ivor. **The Ballet of the Second Empire (1847–
      1858).** London: Black, 1955, pp. 33-37. Citation
      also used following items 281 and 402, and pre-
      ceding items 280 and 285.
      GV 1649.G79

      On the history of **Griseldis**.

LA FILLEULE DES FÉES

*   Beaumont, Cyril W. **Complete Book of Ballets,**
      pp. 341-49. Cited above as item 75.

      History and plot.

*   ———. **Complete Book of Ballets,** pp. 280-86.
      Cited above as item 76.

      History and plot.

*   Guest, Ivor. **The Ballet of the Second Empire (1847–
      1858),** pp. 47-50. Cited above as item 279.

      On the history of **La filleule des fées**.

280. Krasovskaĭa, Vera Mikhaĭlovna. **Russkiĭ baletnyĭ teatr ot vozniknoveniĭa do serediny XIX veka.** Leningrad: Iskusstvo, 1958, pp. 231–43.

About Jules Perrot, choreographer of **La filleule des fées.**

281. Saint–Georges, Jules Henri Vernoy de, and Jules Perrot. **La filleule des fées: Grand ballet–féerie en 3 actes et 7 tableaux, précedé d'un prologue.** Paris: Ve. Jonas, 1849.

Scenario.

ORFA

* Guest, Ivor. **The Ballet of the Second Empire (1847–1858),** pp. 67–68. Cited above as item 279.

On the history of **Orfa.**

* ———— . **Fanny Cerrito.** Cited above as item 217.

Biography of the ballerina, with some material on **Orfa.**

282. Trianon, Henry, and Joseph Mazilier. **Orfa.** Paris: M. Lévy Frères, 1958.

Scenario.

283. ———— . **Orfa (légende islandaise du huitième siècle): Ballet–pantomime en deux actes.** Paris: Michel–Lévy, 1853.

Scenario.

RILLA

284. Petipa, Lucien. **Rilla, ossia, Le fate di provenza: Ballo grande in un prologo e quattro quadri.** Milan: Tip. di P.R. Carpano, 1855.

Scenario. Only mention of the ballet is in item 58.

LE CORSAIRE

(See also **Celebration** and **Le jardin animé**)

1. History, plots, other general works

* Balanchine, George. **Balanchine's New Complete Stories of the Great Ballets,** pp. 103–04. Cited above as i

item 88.

History and plot.

*   Balanchine, George, and Francis Mason. **Balanchine's
     Complete Stories of the Great Ballets,** pp. 99,
     143–44. Cited above as item 89.

     History and plot of **Le corsaire** (pages 143 and
     144) and the use of the pas de deux from **Le corsaire**
     in the ballet **Celebration** (page 99).

*   Beaumont, Cyril W. **Ballet Design, Past and Present.**
     Cited above as item 94.

     This well-illustrated treatise on ballet sets and
     costumes includes material on **Le corsaire.**

*   ———. **Complete Book of Ballets,** pp. 253–65. Cited
     above as item 75.

     History and plot.

*   ———. **Complete Book of Ballets,** pp. 208–18. Cited
     above as item 76.

     History and plot.

*   Clarke, Mary, and Clement Crisp. **The Ballet Goer's
     Guide,** p. 202. Cited above as item 106.

     History and plot of **Le corsaire pas de deux.**

*   Guest, Ivor. **The Ballet of the Second Empire (1847–
     1858),** pp. 96–101. Cited above as item 279.

     On the history of **Le corsaire.**

285. ———. **The Ballet of the Second Empire (1858–1870).**
     London: Black, 1953, pp. 102–04.
     GV 1649.G8

     On the history of **Le corsaire** and its 1867 revival.

286. Koegler, Horst. "The Zagreb Ballet on the Lake Stage
     at the Bregenz Festival: A Lakeside Corsair."
     Dance and Dancers 26 (October 1975): 36–37.

     On a performance of **Le corsaire** in a full version.
     The author admires "this lovable ballet monster."

* Martin, John Joseph. "Reports from Russia." Cited above as item 140.

  Has some material on the Russian production of **Le corsaire.**

* Rebling, Eberhard. **Ballet von A bis Z,** pp. 208–11. Cited above as item 147.

  Plot and discussion of **Le corsaire.**

* Reynolds, Nancy, and Susan Reimer-Torn. **In Performance,** pp. 37–39. Cited above as item 149.

  History and plot of **Le corsaire pas de deux.**

* **The Simon and Schuster Book of the Ballet,** pp. 123–24. Cited above as item 79.

  History and plot.

287. "The Sitter Out: Ivor Guest has written..." **Dancing Times,** no. 550 (July 1956): 561–62.

  Brief but informative essay on the first performance of **Le corsaire** and the ballet's subsequent history.

* **100 [Sto] baletnykh libretto,** pp. 25–29. Cited above as item 158.

  History and plot.

* Terry, Walter. **Ballet Guide,** pp. 99–100. Cited above as item 160.

  History and plot.

2.   Scenarios

288. Ronzani, Domenico. **Il corsaro: Ballo in due atti e cinque quadri.** Turin: D. Ronzani, [ca. 1840].

  This is the same basic scenario as item 289 (an Italian version of **Le corsaire,** using Adam's music). This scenario, however, was written for a ca. 1840 production which used music by another composer.

289. ———— . **Il corsaro: Ballo in due atti e cinque quadri.** Milan: R.P. Carpano, 1857.

Scenario for an Italian production of **Le corsaire**, using Adam's music. A similar scenario (item 288) was written for a ca. 1840 production not using Adam's music.

290. Saint-Georges, Jules Henri Vernoy de, and Joseph Mazilier. **Le corsaire.** Paris: Ve. Jonas, 1867.

Scenario published on the occasion of an 1867 revival.

291. ———— . **Le corsaire: Ballet-pantomime en trois actes.** Paris: Ve. Jonas, 1856.

Scenario.

3.   Dancers and dance companies in relation to **Le corsaire**

*   Bland, Alexander. **The Nureyev Image.** Cited above as item 200.

Photo-biography of the dancer, including material on his performance in **Le corsaire**.

292. Karsavina, Tamara. **Teatral'naĭa uliṫsa.** Leningrad: Iskusstvo, 1971, pp. 163–67.
GV 1785.K3 A317

On her performance in **Le corsaire**. This is the Russian translation of **Theater Street** (item 293).

293. ———— . **Theater Street: The Reminiscences of Tamara Karsavina.** New York: Dutton, 1931, pp. 219–26.
GV 1785.K3 A3 1931

On her performance in **Le corsaire**. In the revised edition (New York: Dutton, 1961), see pages 179–184.

*   Money, Keith. **Fonteyn, the Making of a Legend,** pp. 212–13. Cited above as item 235.

On the ballerina's performance in **Le corsaire pas de deux.**

*   Smakov, Gennady. **Baryshnikov.** Cited above as item 238.

Biography of the dancer, with material on his performance in **Le corsaire.**

4.   Movies

* Braun, Susan, and Jessie Kitching, comps. **Dance and Mime Film and Videotape Catalog**, p. 33. Cited above as item 241.

    Annotation on a movie version of **Le corsaire pas de deux.**

* Mueller, John. **Dance Film Directory**, p. 39. Cited above as item 242.

    Evaluation of a movie version of **Le corsaire pas de deux.**

KATERINA

* Beaumont, Cyril W. **Complete Book of Ballets,** pp. 1044–49. Cited above as item 75.

    History and plot.

* ———— . **Complete Book of Ballets,** pp. 857–61. Cited above as item 76.

    History and plot.

294. Lawson, Joan. "A Short History of Soviet Ballet, 1917–1943." **Dance Index** 2 (June–July 1943): 77–96.

    Includes a brief description of **Katerina.**

* L'vov-Anokhin, B. **Galina Ulanova,** pp. 163–66. Cited above as item 228.

    On the ballerina's performance in **Katerina.**

GISELLE'S REVENGE

295. Barzel, Ann. "Tampa: Florida Ballet Theatre." **Dance Magazine** 54 (April 1980): 100, 102.

    On the performance of **Giselle's Revenge.**

296. McDonagh, Don. **The Complete Guide to Modern Dance.** Garden City, N.Y.: Doubleday, 1976, pp. 188–89.
    GV 1783.M26   ISBN 0385050550

    History and plot.

PAS DE DEUX FOR FOUR

297. Moore, Lillian. "Manhattan Festival Ballet, at
      Theatre 80, St. Marks Place, N.Y., Feb. 6." **Dance
      News** 50 (March 1967): 10.

      On the premiere performance of **Pas de Deux for Four.**

CELEBRATION

*   Balanchine, George, and Francis Mason. **Balanchine's
      Complete Stories of the Great Ballets,** pp. 99-101.
      Cited above as item 89.

      History and plot.

*   _____ . **101 Stories of Great Ballets,** pp. 46-48.
      Cited above as item 90.

      History and plot.

L'AIR D'ESPRIT

298. Baker, Rob. "The Joffrey Ballet (City Center, 55th
      Street Theater, Apr. 5-30)." **Dance Magazine** 52
      (July 1978): 35-36, 38, 40, 89.

      Includes brief material on the performance of
      L'air d'esprit.

299. Barnes, Patricia. "Joffrey Ballet at New York City
      Center: A Year of Activity." **Dance and Dancers** 30
      (March 1979): 38, 40.

      Contains an informative brief section on the
      history and performance of **L'air d'esprit.**

300. Barzel, Ann. "Chicago." **Dance News** 43
      (March 1978): 7.

      Includes a brief passage about the performance of
      L'air d'esprit.

301. _____ . "Chicago." **Dance News** 43 (April 1978): 17.

      Includes material on the performance of **L'air
      d'esprit.**

302. Dunning, Jennifer. "The Spirit of Spessivtzeva
      Inspires a New Pas de Deux." **New York Times**
      (April 2, 1978).

On the performance of **L'air d'esprit.**

303. Goldner, Nancy. "Joffrey Ballet, City Center,
     New York, April 5-30, 1978." **Dance News** 43
     (June 1978): 13.

     Includes material on the performance of **L'air
     d'esprit.**

LE JARDIN ANIMÉ

304. Anderson, Jack. "New York Newsletter." **Dancing Times**
     no. 850 (July 1981): 686-87.

     Includes brief material on the performance of
     Le jardin animé.

305. Goldner, Nancy. "American Ballet Theatre, Petipa
     Program, Metropolitan Opera House, April 20-
     June 13." **Dance News** 47 (September 1981): 13.

     Includes commentary on the performance of **Le
     jardin animé.**

ADAM'S OPERAS IN GENERAL

306. Clément, Félix, and Pierre Larousse. **Dictionnaire des
     opéras (Dictionnaire lyrique).** Paris: Admini-
     stration de grand dictionnaire universel, 1881.

     Contains short articles on several of Adam's
     operas. This is a revised edition of **Dictionnaire
     lyrique** (item 307). Other editions were published in
     1897, 1905, and 1969.

307. ────. **Dictionnaire lyrique, ou, Histoire des
     opéras.** Paris: Administration du grand diction-
     naire universel, 1869.
     ML 102.06 C42 1869

     Contains short articles on several of Adam's
     operas. The revised edition was published under
     title: **Dictionnaire des opéras** (item 306).

308. Cooper, Martin. "Before Broadway: Musical Comedy Has
     an Ancestor in Opera Comique." **Opera News** 30
     (April 9, 1966): 9-12.

     Tells how French comic opera contributed to the
     development of musical comedy. Pages 11-12 deal with
     Adam's significant part in the development.

309. Drone, Jeanette Marie. **Index to Opera, Operetta, and
     Musical Comedy Synopses in Collections and
     Periodicals.** Metuchen, N.J.: Scarecrow Press,
     1978. Citation also used following items 326, 374,
     and 383.
     ML 128.04 D76   ISBN 0810811006

     Indexes 78 English language publications (74 books,
     4 periodicals) which have plots of operas and
     operettas. Some of the publications indexed are included
     in this bibliography under the individual opera. The
     works by Adam which are covered are **Le postillon de
     Lonjumeau, La poupée de Nuremberg,** and **Si
     j'étais roi.**

310. Hughes, Gervase. **Composers of Operetta.** London:
     Macmillan, 1962, pp. 11-16.
     ML 390.H887 C59

     Very good review of Adam's light operas, with
     musical examples. Another edition was published in
     1962 by St. Martin's, New York.

311. Loewenberg, Alfred, comp. **Annals of Opera, 1597–
     1940.** 3d ed. Totowa N.J.: Rowman and
     Littlefield, 1978.
     ML 102.06 L6 1978   ISBN 0874718511

     Outstanding reference book on opera, with a
     detailed record of production, as well as other
     historical data. Fifteen of Adam's operas are
     included. Other editions were published in 1943,
     1955, and 1970.

312. Mackinlay, Sterling. **Origin and Development of Light
     Opera.** Philadelphia: D. McKay, 1927, pp. 105-06,
     108-09.
     ML 1850.M3

     Pages 108-109 are on Adam's contribution to comic
     opera, where "his talent shone most highly." The
     author is generally negative about Adam's music,
     stating that "sometimes his melodies are trivial in
     the extreme; his structure of concerted pieces is of
     the flimsiest kind; his dance rhythms are used with-
     out moderation." Included is some short but worth-
     while biographical material about Theodor Wachtel, who
     was made famous by his performances in **Le postillon
     de Lonjumeau.** Pages 105-106 tell the story of how
     Adam and Theodore Labarre assisted Boieldieu with the

composition of **La dame blanche,** with both of Boieldieu's pupils contributing several parts.

313. Mattfeld, Julius. **A Handbook of American Operatic Premieres, 1731–1962.** Detroit: Information Service, Inc., 1963.
ML 128.04 M3

Gives place, date, and sometimes other data on the American premieres of nine of Adam's operas.

314. Soubies, Albert. **Histoire du Théâtre–Lyrique, 1851–1870.** Paris: Fischbacher, 1899.
ML 1727.8.P2 S7

History of the Théâtre–Lyrique from 1851 to 1870, with a useful chart listing performance dates, authors, and number of performances for operas performed at that theater. Included in the chart are several of Adam's operas.

315. Soubies, Albert, and Charles Halherbe. **Histoire de L'Opéra Comique: La second Salle Favart, 1840–1887.** 2 vols. Paris: Libraire Marpon et Flammarion, 1892–93.
ML 1727.8.P2 S73

History of the Opéra Comique from 1840 to 1887, with much valuable historical material on Adam's operas.

316. ———— . **Histoire de L'Opéra Comique: La second Salle Favart, 1840–1887.** 2 vols. Geneva: Minkoff reprint, 1978.
ML 1727.8.P2 S73 1978   ISBN 2826606298

Reprint of item 315.

317. Traubner, Richard. **Operetta: A Theatrical History.** Garden City, N.Y.: Doubleday, 1983, pp. 5–6. Citation also used following item 324.

Short but well-done section on Adam's contributions to operetta.

318. Walsh, T.J. **Second Empire Opera: The Théâtre Lyrique, Paris, 1851–1870.** London: J. Calder, 1981.
ML 1727.8.P2 W3 1981   ISBN 0714536598

Valuable data on Adam's operas of the period, including a chronology of the theater's repertory and an

index by composer of the operas performed at the
theater.

INDIVIDUAL OPERAS

LE CALEB DE WALTER SCOTT

319. Mitchell, Jerome. **The Walter Scott Operas: An
      Analysis of Operas based on the Works of Sir Walter
      Scott.** University, Ala.: University of Alabama
      Press, 1977, pp. 105–11.
      ML 80.S37 M6   ISBN 0817364013

      History, plot, and musical themes.

LE CHALET

320. Bethléem, L. [and others]. **Les opéras, les opéras-
      comiques, et les opérettes.** Paris: Editions de la
      revue de lectures, 1926, p. 62. Citation is also used
      following items 370, 371, 377, and 378.

      History and plot.

321. Pendle, Karin. **Eugène Scribe and French Opera of the
      Nineteenth Century.** Ann Arbor: UMI Research
      Press, 1979, pp. 196–213.
      ML 1727.P37   ISBN 0835710041

      History and criticism, with 6 musical examples.
      This is the best material on **Le chalet.** The entire
      book on the librettist, in fact, is of value since
      Scribe collaborated with Adam on several occasions.

322. _____ . "The Transformation of a Libretto: Goethe's
      'Jery und Bätely'." **Music and Letters** 55
      (1974): 77–88.

      Very good study on **Le chalet,** comparing it with
      Goethe's work **Jery und Bätely,** from which **Le chalet**
      was adapted.

323. Scribe, Augustin Eugène, and Mélesville [Anne Honoré
      Joseph Duveyrier]. **Le Chalet: Opéra–Comique en un
      Acte.** Paris: Librairie Stock, 1924.

      Libretto.

324. _____ . **The Chalet, or, Caught not Won: A Comic
      Opera in One Act.** [London?, 1852?].

      Libretto.

*   Traubner, Richard. **Operetta,** p. 6. Cited above as
      item 317.

      Short history and plot.

                          LA MARQUISE

325. Saint-Georges, Jules Henri Vernoy de, and Adolphe
      de Leuven. **La marquise: Opéra-comique en un acte.**
      Paris: Marchant, 1835.

      Libretto.

                          MICHELINE

326. Saint-Hilaire, Amable, Michel Masson, and Théodore
      Ferdinand Vallon de Villeneuve. **Micheline, ou,
      L'heure de l'esprit: Opéra-comique en un acte.**
      Paris: Marchant, 1835.

      Libretto.

                   LE POSTILLON DE LONJUMEAU

          1. History, plots, other general works

      (The history and plot materials below, which vary
                in content, were selected from a
                    wide body of literature)

*   Drone, Jeanette Marie. **Index to Opera, Operetta, and
      Musical Comedy Synopses in Collections and
      Periodicals.** Cited above as item 309.

      Indexes publications which have plots of **Le
      postillon de Lonjumeau.** Some of the sources indexed
      are included in this bibliography.

327. "Dusseldorf." **Opera** 20 (February 1969): 149.

      On the performance of **Le postillon de Lonjumeau** in
      Dusseldorf.

328. Eaton, Quaintance. **Opera: A Pictorial Guide.**
      New York: Abaris Books, 1980, p. 9.
      MT 95.E2   ISBN 0913870714

      Plot.

329. _____ . **Opera Production II: A Handbook.** Minne-
      apolis: University of Minnesota Press, 1974, p. 186.

MT 955.E25 1974   ISBN 0816606897

Plot, plus requirements for production of the
opera, including the requirements of the singing
roles.

330. Ewen, David. **The Book of European Light Opera.**
New York: Holt, Rinehart, and Winston, 1962,
pp. 194–95. Citation also used following items
374 and 383.
MT 95.E9

History, plot, and mention of the more important
songs.

*   _____ . **The Complete Book of Classical Music,**
pp. 415–16. Cited above as item 113.

History and plot. A short general essay on Adam is
on pages 414–415.

331. _____ . **The New Encyclopedia of the Opera.**
New York: Hill and Wang, 1971, p. 551.
ML 102.06 E9 1971   ISBN 0809072629

History and plot.

332. Forbes, Elizabeth. "France: 'Postillon' Revived."
Opera 23 (January 1972): 70.

On the performance of **Le postillon de Lonjumeau** in
Marseilles.

333. Harewood, George, ed. **Kobbé's Complete Opera Book.**
New York: Putnam, 1972, pp. 677–79.
MT 95.K52 1972   ISBN 0399110445

History and plot. For a similar edition, see the
1954 edition published by Putnam, New York.

334. _____ . **Kobbé's Complete Opera Book.** London:
Putnam, 1976, pp. 755–57.
MT 95.K52 1976b   ISBN 0370100204

History and plot; same as item 335.

335. _____ . **The New Kobbé's Complete Opera Book.**
New York: Putnam, 1976, pp. 755–57.
MT 95.K52 1976   ISBN 0399116338

History and plot; same as item 334.

336. Howard, John Tasker. **The World's Great Operas.**
     New York: Random House, 1948, pp. 316–17.
     MT 95.H68

          Plot. Another edition was published 1948 by
     Grosset and Dunlap, New York.

337. **Knoch's Opera Guide: Contains Over Two Hundred
     Descriptions of Celebrated Operas with Short
     Biographies of Their Composers.** Vienna:
     R. Lechner, [1927], pp. 402–03. Citation also
     used preceding items 375 and 384.

     Plot.

338. Kobbé, Gustav. **The Complete Opera Book: The Stories
     of the Operas, Together with 400 of the Leading
     Airs and Motives in Musical Notation.** New York:
     Putnam, 1922, pp. 497–98.
     MT 95.K52 1922

     History of the opera, mostly about Theodor Wachtel,
     the singer who was made famous by his role as the
     postillion.

339. Mayer, Anton. **Die Oper.** Berlin: K. Wolff, 1935,
     pp. 372–73.

     Plot.

340. McSpadden, John Walker. **Light Opera and Musical
     Comedy.** New York: Crowell, 1936, pp. 51–52.
     ML 1900.M3 L5

     Very well-written history and plot, listing the
     opera's best-known musical numbers.

341. _____ . **Operas and Musical Comedies.** Enlarged
     ed. New York: Crowell, 1951, pp. 437–38.
     MT 95.M154 1951

     History and plot.

342. Melitz, Leo. **The Opera Goer's Complete Guide:
     Comprising Two Hundred and Nine Opera Plots with
     Musical Numbers and Casts.** Translated by Richard
     Salinger. New York: Dodd Mead, 1908, pp. 305–07.
     Citation also used following item 377.
     MT 95.M3

     Plot.

343. Micheli, Piero. "Readers' Letters: Who Was Rose?"
      Opera 19 (May 1968): 426.

      Letter to the editor concerning who created one of
      the characters in **Le postillon de Lonjumeau.**

344. Moore, Frank Ledlie, cᴏmp. **Crowell's Handbook of
      World Opera.** New York: Crowell, 1961, p. 133.
      ML 102.06 M6

      History and plot.

345. Nodnagel, Ernst Otto, **Der Postillon von Lonjumeau:
      Komische Oper in 3 Aufzügen.** Leipzig: Seeman,
      1901. 31 p.

      Criticism of **Le postillon de Lonjumeau.**

346. Schreiber, Ulrich. "Bielefeld: Höhen-Gesang."
      Opernwelt (June 1967): 44.

      On the performance of **Le postillon de Lonjumeau** in
      Bielefeld.

347. **The Simon and Schuster Book of the Opera: A Complete
      Reference Guide, 1597 to the Present.** New York:
      Simon and Schuster, 1977, pp. 182, 186. Citation
      also used following item 387.
      ML 102.06 063   ISBN 0671248863

      History and plot on page 182, illustration of cos-
      tume on page 186; translation of **L'opera: Répertorio
      della lirica dal 1597.**

348. Slonimsky, Nicolas. "Musical Oddities." **Etude** 73
      (June 1955): 4.

      Short but very useful essay on **Le postillion de
      Lonjumeau** giving the plot plus an anecdote about an
      inn in the town of Longjumeau. The author notes that
      the authorities in the town insist on the "Longjumeau"
      spelling for the opera rather than the "Lonjumeau"
      spelling of the original title.

349. Strantz, Ferdinand von, and Adolf Stauch. **Der grosse
      Opernführer.** Munich: E. Vollmer, 1978, pp. 1-3.
      Citation also used following items 371, 377 and 387.
      MT 95.S895 1978   ISBN 3878760418

      History and plot.

350. Thompson, Oscar. **Plots of the Operas: 266 Stories
      of the Operas.** Cleveland: World Publishing Co.,
      1943, pp. 378-79.
      MT 95.T54 P6 1943

      History and plot. Other editions were published.

351. Upton, George P. **The Standard Light Operas: Their
      Plots and Their Music: A Handbook.** Chicago:
      A.C. McClurg, 1902, pp. 15-18.
      MT 95.U70

      Plot and analysis of the music.

352. _____ . **The Standard Operas: Their Plots and Their
      Music.** Chicago: A.C. McClurg, 1925, pp. 1-3.
      MT 95.U74

      Plot, analysis of the music, and a portrait of
      Theodor Wachtel, who made the title role famous.
      Other editions were also published.

353. Wehnert, M. "Zwei komische Opern." **Musica** 14 (1960):
      155-56.

      On the performance of **Le postillon de Lonjumeau** in
      Leipzig.

354. Westerman, Gerhart von. **Knaurs Opernführer: Eine
      Geschichte de Oper.** New complete ed.
      Munich: Th. Knaur, 1952, pp. 163-65.
      ML 1700.W4 1952

      Plot with one musical theme.

355. _____ . **Opera Guide.** Edited, with an introduction,
      by Harold Rosenthal. Translated by Ann Ross.
      New York: Dutton, 1965, pp. 179-81.
      ML 1700.W42

      Plot with one musical theme. This adaptation of
      item 354 was also published in 1964 by Thames and
      Hudson, London.

*   Winkler, H.J. **Oper und Ballett**, pp. 27-28. Cited
      above as item 169.

      History and plot.

356. Wölfing, Siegmund. "Leipzig." **Opera** 11 (July 1960):
      482-83.

On the performance of **Le postillon de Lonjumeau** in Leipzig.

357. Zimmermann, C. "Aachen." **Oper und Konzert** 14, no. 11 (1976): 6.

On the performance of **Le postillon de Lonjumeau** in Aachen.

2. Librettos

358. À Beckett, Gilbert Abbott. **The Postilion: An Opera in Three Acts.** London: J. Cumberland, [1843?].

Also on microcard (**Nineteenth Century English and American Drama,** no. 435) and also published by G.H. Davidson, London, ca. 1843.

359. Leuven, Adolphe de, and Brunswick [Léon Lévy Lhérie]. **The Postilion of Lonjumeau: A Comic Opera: Der Postillion Von Lonjumeau.** New York: Rullman, 1870.

English and German libretto.

360. _____ . **Postilion of Lonjumeau: A Comic Opera in Three Acts.** Boston: O. Ditson, [18--].

361. _____ . **Le postillon de Longjumeau: Opéra-comique en trois actes.** Paris: Marchant, 1837.

362. _____ . **Der Postillon de Lonjumeau: Komische Oper in 3 Akten.** Wiesbaden: W. Friedrich'sche Buchdruckerei, 1859.

363. _____ . **Le postillon de Lonjumeau: Opéra comique en trois actes.** Paris: Barba, 1836.

364. _____ . **Postillon från Lonjumeau: Komedi med sång i tre akter.** Stockholm: Hörbergska Boktryckeriet, 1838.

365. _____ . **The Postillon of Lonjumeau: A Comic Opera in Three Acts.** [London?, 1852?].

3. Derivatives, adaptations, etc.

366. Carcassi, Matteo. **Fantaisie sur les motifs du Postillon de Lonjumeau d'Ad. Adam, Op. 64.** Mainz: B. Schotts Söhne, [192-].

Guitar adaptation of music from **Le postillon de Lonjumeau.**

LE BRASSEUR DE PRESTON

367. Leuven, Adolphe de, and Brunswick [Léon Lévy Lhérie]. **Le brasseur de Preston: Opera comique en trois actes.** Paris: Marchant, 1838.

Libretto.

LA REINE D'UN JOUR

368. Fitzwilliam, Edward. **The Queen of a Day: A Comic Opera in Two Acts: Produced for the First Time in America by the Pyne and Harrison English Opera Troupe.** Boston: J.H. Eastburn's Press, 1855.

Adaption of Adam's **La reine d'un jour,** with additional music by Fitzwilliam.

LE ROI D'YVETOT

369. Leuven, Adolphe de, and Brunswick [Léon Lévy Lhérie]. **Le roi d'Yvetot: Opéra—comique en trois actes.** Paris: Marchant, 1842.

Libretto.

LES PREMIERS PAS

370. Royer, Alphonse, and Gustave Vaëz [Jean Nicholas Nieuwenhuysen]. **Les premiers pas: Opéra comique en un acte.** Poissy: Imp. G. Olivier, 1847.

Libretto.

LE TORÉADOR

* Bethléem, L. [and others]. **Les opéras, les opéras-comiques, et les opérettes,** p. 62. Cited above as item 320.

History and plot.

371. Sauvage, Thomas Marie François. **Le toréador, ou, L'accord parfait: Opéra bouffon en deux actes.** Paris: Dondey-Dupre, [1849?].

Libretto.

*   Strantz, Ferdinand von, and Adolf Stauch. **Der grosse Opernführer**, p. 6. Cited above as item 349.

       History and plot.

GIRALDA

*   Bethléem, L. [and others]. **Les opéras, les opéras-comiques, et les opérettes**, pp. 62–63. Cited above as item 320.

       History and plot.

372.   Burgmueller, Johann Friedrich Franz. **Giralda, opéra d'Ad. Adam: Valse brillante pour piano.** Boston: Ditson, [185–?].

       Waltz adapted from **Giralda**.

373.   Ettling, Émile. **Suite de valses sur Giralda, opéra d'Adam.** Paris: Brandus & cie., 1850.

       Suite of waltzes adapted from **Giralda**.

374.   Scribe, Augustin Eugène. **Giralda, o, El marido misterioso: Zarzuela en tres actos, en verso, arreglada a la escena española.** Madrid: Vidua e hijos de J. Cuesta, 1862.

       Libretto.

LA POUPÉE DE NUREMBERG

*   Drone, Jeanette Marie. **Index to Opera, Operetta and Musical Comedy Synopses in Collections and Periodicals.** Cited above as item 309.

       Indexes publications which have plots of **La poupée de Nuremberg**. Some of the sources indexed are included in this bibliography.

*   Ewen, David. **The Book of European Light Opera**, pp. 195–96. Cited above as item 330.

       History, plot, and mention of the more important songs.

*   **Knoch's Opera Guide**, pp. 360–61. Cited above as item 337.

       Plot.

375. Leuven, Adolphe de, and Victor Arthur Rousseau de
     Beauplan. **Le poupée de Nuremberg: Opéra-comique en
     un acte.** Paris: D. Giraud et J. Dagneau, 1852.

     Libretto.

376. ───── . **Die Nurnberger Puppe: Komische Oper in 1 Act.**
     Mainz: B. Schott's Söhne [192-?].

     Libretto.

377. Loskill, Joerg. "In der kürze Liegt der Opernwürze."
     Opernwelt 19, no. 11 (1978): 56.

     On the performance of **La poupée de Nuremberg.**

*   Melitz, Leo. **The Opera Goer's Complete Guide,** p. 272.
     Cited above as item 342.

     Plot.

*   Strantz, Ferdinand von, and Adolf Stauch. **Der grosse
     Opernführer,** pp. 3-4. Cited above as item 349.

     History and plot.

                        LE FARFADET

*   Bethléem, L. [and others]. **Les opéras, les opéras-
     comiques, et les opérettes,** p. 63. Cited above as
     item 320.

     History and plot.

                       SI J'ÉTAIS ROI

378. Asche, Gerhardt. "Konventionell: Adams Wenn ich König
     wär in Braunschweig." **Opernwelt** 22, no. 8-9
     (August/September 1981): 72-73.

     On the performance of **Si j'étais roi** in
     Braunschweig.

*   Bethléem. L. [and others]. **Les opéras, les opéras-
     comiques, et les operettes,** pp. 63-65. Cited
     above as item 320.

     History and plot.

379. **Composers' Autographs: Volume 2, from Schubert to
     Stravinsky.** Madison [N.J.]: Fairleigh Dickinson
     University Press, 1968, pp. 12, 164.

Page 12 is a reproduction of the manuscript of **Si j'étais roi,** and page 164 is a description of the manuscript. Another edition was published in 1968 by Cassell, London.

380. Crichton, Ronald. "If I Were King: John Lewis Music Society, London." **Opera** 32 (July 1981):   759-60.

On the performance of **Si j'étais roi** in England.

381. Dean, Winton. "Si j'étais roi." **The Musical Times** 122 (June 1981):   404.

On the performance of **Si j'étais roi** in England.

382. DelBonta, Robert J. "Songs of India." **Opera Quarterly** 2, no. 1 (1984):   5-14.

On the influence of India on western musical works, including **Si j'étais roi.**

383. D'Ennery, Adolphe Philippe [Adolphe Philippe], and Jules Brésil. **Si j'étais roi: Opéra comique en trois actes et quatre tableaux.** New Orleans: L. Fiot, [ca. 1860].

French and English libretto.

*   Drone, Jeanette Marie. **Index to Opera, Operetta and Musical Comedy Synopses in Collections and Periodicals.** Cited above as item 309.

Indexes publications which have plots of **Si j'étais roi.** Some of the sources indexed are included in this bibliography.

*   Ewen, David. **The Book of European Light Opera,** pp. 221-22. Cited above as item 330.

History, plot and mention of the more important music.

*   _____ . **The Complete Book of Classical Music,** p. 417. Cited above as item 113.

Plot plus analysis of the music of the overture. A short general essay on Adam is on pages 414-415.

*   **Knoch's Opera Guide,** pp. 244-46. Cited above as item 337.

Plot.

384. Koch, Heinz. "Zu sagen hat er nichts Adams Wenn ich
     König wär in Freiburg." **Opernwelt** 17, no. 6
     (June 1976): 35-36.

     On the performance of **Si j'étais roi** in Freiburg.

385. Marshall, William. "Aachen." **Opera** 8 (December
     1957): 772.

     On the performance of **Si j'étais roi** in Aachen.

386. Schmidt-Garre, Helmut. "'Wenn ich König wär' im
     Gärtnerplatztheater." **Neue Zeitschrift für Musik**
     122 (October 1961): 411-412.

     On the performance of **Si j'étais roi** in Munich.

387. Schreiber, Ulrich. "Bonn: Fest der Stimmen."
     Opernwelt (May 1967): 45.

     On the performance of **Si j'étais roi** in Bonn.

*   **The Simon and Schuster Book of the Opera,** p. 221.
     Cited above as item 347.

     Brief history.

*   Stranz, Ferdinand von, and Adolf Stauch. **Der grosse
     Opernführer,** pp. 4-5. Cited above as item 349.

     History and plot.

388. Stuckenschmidt, Hans Heinz. "Untraditional
     'passion'." **Musical America** 80 (May 1960): 9-10.

     On the performance of **Si j'étais roi** in Berlin.

*   Winkler, H.J. **Oper und Ballett,** pp. 29-30.
     Cited above as item 169.

     History and plot.

LE ROI DES HALLES

389. Leuven, Adolphe de, and Brunswick [Léon Lévy Lhérie].
     Le roi des Halles: Opéra-comique en trois actes.
     Paris: J. Dagneau, 1853.

     Libretto.

LE BIJOU PERDU

390. Leuven, Adolphe de, and P.A.A. Pittaud de Forges.
      Le bijou perdu: Opéra comique en trois actes.
      Paris: M. Lévy Frères, 1853.

      Libretto.

À CLICHY

391. D'Ennery, Adolphe Philippe [Adolphe Philippe], and
      Eugène Grangé [Eugène Pierre Basté]. **A Clichy:**
      Episode de la vie d'artiste: Opéra—comique en un
      acte. Paris: M. Lévy Frères, [1854?].

      Libretto.

LE HOUZARD DE BERCHINI

392. Rosier, Joseph Bernard. **Le housard de Berchini:**
      Opéra comique en deux actes. Paris: M. Lévy
      Frères, 1855.

      Libretto.

393. Scudo, Paul. **Critique et littérature musicales.** 3d
      ed. Paris: Hachette, 1856–59, vol. 2, pp. 72–73.

      Has contemporary commentary on "Hussard de
      Berchini."

LES PANTINS DE VIOLETTE

394. Battu, Léon. **Les pantins de Violette: Opérette—**
      bouffe en un acte. Paris: M. Lévy Frères, 1859.

      Libretto.

OTHER WORKS

CANTIQUE DE NOËL

395. Bachelin, Henri. "A propos du Noël d'Adam."
      Menestrel 93 (1931): 533–35.

      Excellent essay defending **Cantique de Noël** from
      its critics, stating that the detractors of the carol
      do not base their negativism on artistic criteria, but
      instead on the personal backgrounds of the composer
      and the poet. According to Bachelin, the song is
      refuted because Adam was Jewish and Placide Cappeau,
      author of the lyrics, was a Free—mason and an alleged

social radical.

396. ———— . **Les Noëls français.** Paris: Editions musicales de France, 1927, pp. 64–77.

Best historical material on **Cantique de Noël.** Much space is devoted to the eccentric life of Placide Cappeau, the author of the lyrics.

397. Hervé, Noël. **Les Noëls français: Essai historique et littéraire.** Niort: Librairie L. Clouzot, 1905, pp. 134–136.

Very good historical material on **Cantique de Noël,** though not as comprehensive as item 396. Much of the material is on the lyricist, Placide Cappeau. There is a good brief description of the essence of Adam's music for the carol.

398. Hess, Charles. **Nocturne sur le Noël de Ad. Adam, pour piano, op. 36.** Paris: Grus, [187?].

Piano work adapted from **Cantique de Noël.**

399. Pieyre, Adolphe. "Le Noël d'Adam." **Revue du midi** (May 1, 1899).

Claims that Placide Cappeau, the lyricist, was not a Christian but instead was a free thinker and socialist.

400. Poorter, P. de. "Le Minuit chrétiens?" **Musica sacra "Sancta sancte"** 60 (1959): 147–55.

Emotional essay by a cleric condemning both music and lyrics of **Cantique de Noël,** supposedly on theological and artistic grounds, thus justifying its removal from church services.

401. Studwell, William E. "Cantique de Noël." **Journal of Church Music** 22 (December 1980): 2–4.

Comprehensive article on the historical background and cultural impact of Adam's carol. This is the only known English-language article.

402. ———— . **Christmas Carols: A Reference Guide.** New York: Garland Publishing, 1985, p. 35. ML 102.C3 S9 1985 ISBN 0824088999

Brief reference data on the carol, including

authorship of lyrics and music, date and place of
creation, variant French titles, English trans-
lations, and date of first publication.

LES NATIONS

*   Guest, Ivor. **The Ballet of the Second Empire
       (1847–1858)**, pp. 56–57. Cited above as item 279.

       On the history of **Les nations.**

GENERAL INFORMATION

RESEARCH LACUNAE

There are several areas associated with the life and works of Adam which definitely need further research and publication. First, the only full biography of Adam was published in 1877. Another full biography is much overdue. In addition there has been no full biography in English. Second, there is no literature which comprehensively and in detail treats either Adam's ballets as a group or his operas as a group. Third, an open-minded comprehensive analysis of his music is needed. Fourth, most of his individual works have not received sufficient coverage. **Giselle**, of course, has been favored by much literature. But most of the rest of his works of consequence have not been given sufficient attention. Two exceptions are Karin Pendle's scholarly work on **Le chalet** and the literature on **Cantique de Noël** produced by Henri Bachelin and others. Works which should also be studied more because they are still performed and/or are of historical interest include the operas **Le postillon de Lonjumeau, La poupée de Nuremberg,** and **Si j'étais roi** and the ballets **La jolie fille de Gand, Le diable à quatre, La filleule des fées,** and **Le corsaire.**

LIBRARY RESOURCES FOR RESEARCH

Three collections contain significant material for research on Adam. One is the New York Public Library's splendid comprehensive dance collection which has a large amount of books, periodicals, films, illustrations, clippings, ephemera, etc. on Adam's ballets, and on Adam in general. The other two are the excellent resources of the Département de la Musique, Bibliothèque nationale, Paris, and of the Bibliothèque de L'Opéra, Paris.

PERSONAL AND PLACE NAME DICTIONARY

Adam, Jean Louis (1758-1848): father of Adolphe and pianist, teacher, and composer. He tried to discourage his son from becoming a musician.

Albert (1789-1865): French dancer and choreographer whose real name was François Decombe. Some sources state his name

was Ferdinand Albert Decombe. He was the co-scenarist and
choreographer for **La jolie fille de Gand** and **The Marble
Maiden.**

Albrecht: principal male character in **Giselle.** He is the
Duke of Silesia, who, disguised as a peasant called "Loys",
is developing a love relationship with Giselle, a peasant
girl. When Giselle becomes aware of Albrecht's deception,
she goes mad and kills herself. Later, when Albrecht visits
Giselle's grave in the woods, Giselle, because of her strong
love, saves Albrecht from being a victim of the Wilis, who
would have forced him to dance until dead from exhaustion.

Auber, Daniel François Esprit (1782–1871): French composer
and associate of Adam. He was one of the most successful
composers of operatic works of the second quarter of the
nineteenth century, and was one of Adam's chief predecessors
in light opera.

Beatrice (or Beatrix): principal female character in **La
jolie fille de Gand,** betrothed to Benedict.

Bénédict: principal male character in **La jolie fille de
Gand,** betrothed to Beatrice. In an Italian variation of the
ballet, which has the title **Beatrice di Gand,** he is called
Benedetto.

Berlioz, Hector (1803–1869): noted French composer and
associate of Adam, whose music was neither understood nor
appreciated by Adam.

Boieldieu, François Adrien (1775–1834): Adam's teacher of
composition and close friend. In 1825 Adam helped Boieldieu
with the composition of **La dame blanche.** Together with
Daniel Auber, Boieldieu and Adam were the chief figures in
French opéra–comique during the first half of the nineteenth
century and somewhat beyond.

Brunswick (1805–1859): pseudonym of Léon Lévy Lhérie, co-
librettist (usually with Adolphe de Leuven) of five of
Adam's operas, notably **Le postillon de Lonjumeau.**

Cappeau, Placide (1808–1877): author of the lyrics of
Cantique de Noël. He was an eccentric from the south of
France who is known for nothing else, and except for a
mutual acquaintance would never have contacted Adam to
supply the music for the carol.

Chappelou: the coachman and title character in **Le postillon
de Lonjumeau.** He is a fine singer who leaves his bride Made-
line to become the principal tenor at the Paris Opéra. In the
end, after the usual array of confusion, the couple is reunited.

Conrad: the title character in **Le corsaire.** He is a pirate who falls in love with Medora, a Greek girl who is sold into slavery. After rescuing Medora from the pasha who bought her and wants to marry her, Conrad escapes with Medora on a ship which is sunk by a storm. The couple, however, miraculously survives.

Coralli, Jean (1779–1854): Italian dancer and choreographer (originally J.C. Peracini), who with Jules Perrot choreographed the initial version of **Giselle,** and who quite possibly helped write the scenario.

Delibes, Léo (1836–1891): noted French composer and pupil of Adam. Because his own father had died in 1847, Delibes probably regarded his mentor Adam as a substitute father. Adam helped Delibes get his first professional positions, and the master's ballets probably influenced the pupil's great ballets (**Coppélia** and **Sylvia**).

D'Ennery, Adolphe Philippe (1811–1899): co-librettist for four of Adam's operas, including **Si j'étais roi.** His real name was Adolphe Philippe.

Gautier, Théophile (1811–1872): French writer who derived the concept for **Giselle** from Heinrich Heine, and who co-authored the libretto.

Germany: Adam has several associations with Germany: his father, Jean Louis Adam, was born there; the locale for **Giselle** is in Germany; he composed an opera-ballet **Die Hamadryaden** while visiting there in 1840; and he had a long correspondence (1836–1850) with a Berlin librarian named Spiker.

Ghent (or Gand): city in Belgium which is the home town of the principal characters of **La jolie fille de Gand,** Beatrice and Bénédict.

Giselle: principal female character in the ballet of that name. When the peasant girl Giselle finds that she has been deceived by Albrecht, with whom she is deeply in love, she becomes insane and kills herself. Later though, Giselle—now one of the night-dancing Wilis—saves Albrecht from death. The Giselle role is considered to be one of the most difficult in the repertory, and also one of the most sought after.

Grisi, Carlotta (1819–1899): renowned dancer of Italian birth who created the ballerina roles in **Giselle, La jolie fille de Gand, Le diable à quatre, Griseldis,** and **La filleule des fées.**

Halévy, Jacques François Fromental Elias (1799–1862):
French composer whose original surname was Levy. In
addition to being a professional associate and collaborator
on the 1847 operatic work **Les premiers pas,** Halévy was one
of Adam's closest friends. He gave a funeral address for
Adam in 1856, and published a posthumous essay on Adam in
1859 (also published in 1861).

Heine, Heinrich (1797–1856): famous German writer whose
book **De l'Allemagne** (1835) gave Théophile Gautier the inspiration for **Giselle.**

Hérold, Louis Joseph Ferdinand (1791–1833): French composer
whose influence was instrumental in Adam's decision to become
a composer.

Hilarion: rival to Albrecht for Giselle's affections in
Giselle. Toward the end of the ballet, Hilarion is forced
to dance to his death by the phantom Wilis, of which Giselle
has become a member.

Leuven, Adolphe de (1800–1884): co-librettist for eleven of
Adam's operas, notably **Le postillon de Lonjumeau** and **La
poupée de Nuremberg,** and co-scenarist for **Le diable à quatre.**

London: Adam had an affinity for England and produced two
ballets (**Faust** and **The Marble Maiden**) and two operatic works
(**His First Campaign** and **The Dark Diamond**) in London. All of
the above works except **The Marble Maiden** were produced
during a period after the 1830 revolution when conditions in
Paris were not favorable for the theater.

Longjumeau: small city about 11 miles south of Paris made
famous by **Le postillon de Lonjumeau.** The original
production of the opera deleted the "g" from the town's
name. A monument in Adam's honor was erected there by the
town's citizens.

Madeleine: principal female character in **Le postillon de
Lonjumeau,** and wife of Chappelou. After her husband has
abandoned her for a singing career in Paris, she inherits a
fortune, assumes the guise of a great lady, and eventually
she and her husband are reunited.

Mazilier, Joseph (1801–1868): French dancer and choreographer (originally Giulio Mazarini) who was the co-
scenarist and choreographer for **Le diable à quatre,
Griseldis, Orfa,** and **Le corsaire.**

Mazourka and Mazourki: principal characters in **Le diable
à quatre,** peasant wife and husband. Mazourka magically
changes identity for a day with a countess, causing much

misunderstanding and confusion.

Medora: principal female character in **Le corsaire**. She is a young Greek girl, sold into slavery, who is in love with the pirate Conrad. Medora is rescued by Conrad from the pasha who bought her and wants to marry her, and the two escape in a ship, miraculously surviving the sinking of the vessel by a storm.

Mélesville (1787-1865): co-librettist with Eugène Scribe of three of Adam's operas, notably **Le chalet**. His real name was Anne Honoré Joseph Duveyrier.

Myrtha: character in **Giselle**. She is Queen of the Wilis, the group of female phantoms who force young men to dance until they are dead.

Offenbach, Jacques (1819-1880): noted French composer, primarily of operettas, and associate of Adam. He was a principal successor to Adam in light theatrical music.

Perrot, Jules Joseph (1810-1882): prominent French dancer and choreographer who, with Jean Coralli, did the choreography for the original version of **Giselle** and who also choreographed **La filleule des fées** and co-authored its scenario.

Roquemaure: small city a few miles north of Avignon, France, which was made famous by one of its residents, Placide Cappeau, who wrote the lyrics for **Cantique de Noël**.

Russia: Adam has two associations with Russia: his ballet Morskoĭ razboĭnik was first performed there in 1840; and Russia has been, over the years, an especially receptive place for Adam's ballets.

Saint-Georges, Jules Henri Vernoy de (1801?-1875): French writer who co-authored the scenarios for five of Adam's ballets (**Giselle, La jolie fille de Gand, The Marble Maiden, La filleule des fées**, and **Le corsaire**) and authored or co-authored the librettos for seven of Adam's operatic works. He was the librettist for Adam's first significant operatic work (**Pierre et Catherine**) in 1829 and scenarist for Adam's last ballet (**Le corsaire**) in 1856.

Scribe, Augustin Eugène (1791-1861): French writer who authored or co-authored the librettos for ten of Adam's operatic works, including **Le chalet** and **Giralda**.

Spiker: A Berlin librarian under Frederick William III and Frederick William IV who corresponded with Adam from 1836 to 1850. Adam's part of this correspondence has been preserved and is a fine resource for material on Adam and the music of his period.

Wachtel, Theodor (1823–1893): German tenor who was made famous and wealthy by his title role in **Le postillon de Lonjumeau,** which he performed over 1,000 times. Because of his exceptional high C and his ability to use a whip in the coachman role, he was very well suited for the part.

NOTABLE PERFORMANCES OTHER THAN PREMIERES

March 13, 1837: Le postillon de Lonjumeau's English premiere in London at St. James's Theatre.

March 30, 1840: Le postillon de Lonjumeau's American debut at Park Theater in New York.

March 12, 1842: Giselle first produced in England at Her Majesty's Theatre, London.

January 17, 1843: the Italian debut of **Giselle** in Milan at the Teatro alla Scala.

March 7, 1845: Beatrice di Gand, a variant version of **La jolie fille de Gand,** first produced at the Teatro alla Scala, Milan.

January, 1858: Le corsaire produced in St. Petersburg at the Bolshoi Theater. The ballet was popular in Russia for decades.

November 12, 1867: at a revival of **Le corsaire** at the Paris Opéra, a divertissement called **Valse, ou, Pas des fleurs** by Léo Delibes was added to the ballet, thus helping to propel Delibes' rising reputation as a ballet composer.

December 24, 1870: an unsubstantiated but plausible occurrence during the Franco–Prussian War. Supposedly, a French soldier came out of the trenches and sang **Cantique de Noël** to the nearby German soldiers, and a German soldier responded with Luther's **Vom Himmel Hoch.**

February 5, 1884: Marius Petipa's production of **Giselle** at the Maryinsky Theater in St. Petersburg. This was not the earliest performance of the ballet in Russia (that was in December 1842), but it was perhaps the most historically and artistically significant.

June 18, 1910: Michael Fokine's production of **Giselle** at the Paris Opéra, with Tamara Karsavina and Vaslav Nijinsky dancing the lead roles.

March 11, 1932: Serge Lifar's production of **Giselle** at the Paris Opéra, with Lifar and Olga Spessivtzeva in the lead roles.

LÉO DELIBES

LÉO DELIBES

OVERVIEW

DELIBES' LIFE AND WORK IN SUMMARY

By no means is the life of every prominent person readily divisible into clear historical periods. Such is the case, though, for Léo Delibes (February 11, 1836–January 16, 1891). The first of four periods is his pre-composition period. Born in the village of Saint-Germain du Val, in the rural Sarthe region of France, Clément Philibert Léo Delibes was raised in a middle class environment. His father, Philibert, who was 53 at Léo's birth, was connected either with the postal service or the stage coach service, and apparently had absolutely no musical background. His mother Clémence, 27 at Léo's birth, was in contrast a skilled musician from a family of Parisian musicians and taught at least the fundamentals of music to her son. In 1847 Léo's father died and the family soon moved to Paris where Léo was enrolled in the Paris Conservatory. Although obviously talented, Léo did not work especially hard at the Conservatory. His professor of composition, Adolphe Adam, became his mentor and quite possibly also a substitute father. In 1853 Léo gained his first professional positions through the influence of Adam. One was as organist at the Church of St. Pierre de Chaillot and the other, in marked contrast, as accompanist at the highly secular Théâtre-Lyrique.

While at the latter, Léo made contacts which led to the start of the second phase of his life, the period of development as a composer (1856–1870). In 1856 he had the opportunity to compose a light operatic work, **Deux sous de charbon**, which was successful. In the next fourteen years he produced over a dozen more light operatic compositions, as well as some other works. Although gaining a degree of success with his early operatic compositions, his first real fame came with the 1866 ballet **La source**, written in collaboration with Léon Minkus. The portions of the work written by the lesser-known Delibes clearly were superior to those by the more-established Minkus, and only Delibes' sections were given much attention in the long run. A year later, Delibes enhanced his reputation as a ballet composer with a highly successful ballet divertissement **Valse, ou, Pas des fleurs** which was added to a revival of Adam's **Le corsaire.**

These two ballet works were preludes to Delibes'
thirteen-year period of triumph. From 1870 to 1883, although
only composing five major works, he produced three long-
lasting masterpieces and another work which is occasionally
performed in the late twentieth century. The first of the
compositions was the ballet **Coppélia**, which was initially
presented on May 25, 1870 at the Paris Opéra. **Coppélia** was
a landmark in Delibes' career and in the history of ballet.
It was Delibes' most popular composition and the one which
brought him the most accolades. In addition, it was the
first ballet to use fully symphonic music and to bring dance
and music together into one unified entity. Because of these
innovations, Delibes is regarded as the first great composer
of ballet music or the "father of modern ballet music." But
Coppélia is not just of historical value. It also is one of
the most beloved and enduring of all ballets and still
stands in the first echelon of the genre.

Coppélia was followed three years later by **Le roi l'a
dit**, Delibes' first important operatic work, which was well
received at its inception and which is still sometimes performed. Three years after, on June 14, 1876, came Delibes'
second masterpiece, the ballet **Sylvia**, which added greatly
to Delibes' reputation as a master of ballet music. **Sylvia**
is inferior to **Coppélia** as a ballet because of a lesser
plot and therefore is not performed as frequently. It remains, however, one of the true classics of the dance due
primarily to its outstanding score which is just as danceable as **Coppélia** but which is more advanced, more sophisticated, and more spiritual. The music of **Sylvia**, in the
judgment of some, may even approach the great scores of
Tchaikovsky's **Swan Lake** and **Sleeping Beauty**.

In 1880 Delibes' most serious opera **Jean de Nivelle**
was produced with some success, though since that time it
has been mostly forgotten. A more lasting success in opera
came on April 14, 1883 with the production of Delibes' third
masterpiece, **Lakmé**. Despite a weak plot, **Lakmé** remains one
of the favorites of the operatic repertory because of its
melodic, colorful, and charming music.

The fourth phase of Delibes life, from 1883 to his
death in 1891, could be called the empty period. In spite
of the considerable success of **Lakmé**, on top of earlier
triumphs, Delibes wrote no major works after **Lakmé** although almost eight years elapsed. He did leave an almost
completed opera **Kassya** which was put into production in 1893
by his friend Jules Massenet. But otherwise, these last
years were as a whole a void. There is no clear or

obvious reason for the emptiness phase, even allowing for
his usual slowness at composition. It is possible though
unlikely that non-composition activities such as his
professorship at the Paris Conservatory (starting in 1881)
took too much time and energy. It is also possible that his
inspiration had run out. But this also is doubtful since
the incomplete score of **Kassya** showed promise[1] but was
doomed to failure by the well-intentioned completion by
Massenet, who had a different musical style, who didn't
supply the missing overture, and whose orchestration
probably varied markedly from what Delibes would have
produced. More likely, Delibes was a victim of his apparent
increasing lack of confidence and/or his easy-going undriven
nature and/or his tendency to be less than diligent in his
work. In any case, his failure to produce other major compositions after **Lakmé** may have deprived the world of one
or two more works of excellence. Therefore we must be
resigned to his lack of quantity while at the same time
appreciating the enduring quality of the ballets and
Lakmé.[2]

DELIBES' RELATIONSHIP TO HIS CONTEMPORARIES

The extremely high regard for Delibes by his contemporaries was shown in several ways. During his life he was
made Chevalier of the Legion of Honor (1877) and was elected
to the prestigious French Institute (1884). After his
death, the tributes posthumously paid to him were numerous.
There were at least two published funeral orations,[3] three
published speeches dedicating a monument to him,[4] and three
memorial essays.[5]

We have very little on Delibes' opinion on his contemporaries, since he left no diary, no great body of letters,
no memoirs. Of his artistic relationships, the most
important are those with his mentor Adolphe Adam and his
Russian colleague Peter Il'ich Tchaikovsky. The relationship with Adam is covered in some detail by the comparable
essay in this book's section on Adolphe Adam.[6] In summary,
Adam guided Delibes in his early years and left him a
significant legacy in ballet.

The relationship with Tchaikovsky is more oblique and
tenuous. The direct personal contact of the two composers
was a very brief one, in the form of an apparently unsatisfying meeting in Paris on June 21, 1886.[7] But in two other
ways their interface was quite significant. First,
Tchaikovsky had an extremely high opinion of Delibes' music,

rating Delibes second only to Bizet among his contemporaries.
There are eight extant letters from 1876 to 1883 documenting
the Russian's great respect for the Frenchman.[8] This admira-
tion can also be inferred by Tchaikovsky's use of ballet
music including a pizzicato in his Fourth Symphony, not long
after he had written laudatory comments about **Sylvia**, which
likewise contained a famous pizzicato. Second, there are
strong indications (but no definite proof) that Tchaikovsky
modeled his great ballets on Delibes' **Coppélia** and **Sylvia**.
Although some historians have claimed that the close sty-
listic similarities between the ballets of the two men were
just coincidence,[9] there is an appreciable amount of opinion
that Tchaikovsky was directly and substantially influenced
by Delibes.[10] The available evidence, though indirect and
circumstantial, definitely tends to support a clear link
between the two. The crucial point in the controversy is
whether Tchaikovsky was acquainted with **Coppélia** prior to
his composition of **Swan Lake** (April 1876). Although
Coppélia was not produced in Russia until 1884, Tchaikovsky may well have had the opportunity to see a performance
of **Coppélia** before 1876. The most promising piece of
data is Tchaikovsky's Paris trip of 1870 when the Russian
lover of dance music twice attended the theater in early
June. At the time **Coppélia**, which was the sensation of the
Parisian musical scene, was being presented at the Opéra,
the city's most illustrious musical theater. In addition,
Tchaikovsky visited Paris three other times before April
1876, all during the long and successful first production of **Coppélia**. It is therefore doubtful that Tchaikovsky
was not familiar with **Coppélia** prior to **Swan Lake**.[11] Even
the initial failure of **Swan Lake** in 1877 may have been in
part due to the strong influence of Delibes on Tchaikovsky
since the more sophisticated Parisian audiences probably
would have been more receptive to the considerable inno-
vation in **Coppélia** than the Russian audiences would have
been to the even more advanced **Swan Lake**.

DELIBES' MUSIC

There is some variance of opinion on Delibes' music.
His ballets (**Coppélia, Sylvia,** and to a lesser extent **La
source**) plus **Lakmé** are generally highly regarded and some of
his other music is given recognition. But the praise given
to Delibes has not been universal. For example, Pierre Lalo
in 1947 felt that "great artist" was a somewhat absurd
appellation for Delibes. At the same time, though, he
described Delibes as a charming, true French musician with
fine, lively works.[12] The non-universality of favorable

treatment for Delibes can also be inferred by Adolphe
Boschot's delight about the return of Delibes to public
attention (1931).[13]

Overall, the majority of commentary on Delibes' music
is of a positive nature. A few examples from different
decades are illustrative of the general pattern. Olin
Downes (1918) extols Delibes as a "master of delicious
ballet music" and describes his perception of the ballet as
"a poem, a dream of most delicate beauty."[14] In the above-
mentioned 1931 essay, Adolphe Boschot as a tribute to
Delibes' music uses the term "Delibes' happy destiny."
An anonymous 1952 British article enthusiastically calls
Sylvia "one of the glories of ballet music."[15] David Ewen
(1961) mentions Delibes' elegance, warm lyricism, richness
of harmonics, and delicacy of orchestration.[16] And with
perhaps the best analysis, Hugh Macdonald (1980) states that
Delibes' "workmanship was of the highest order; he had a
natural gift for harmonic dexterity and a sure sense of
orchestral colour, and nothing in his music is out of place.
He was a disciplined composer."[17]

In the same essay, Macdonald describes Delibes' music
as "melodic." Other historians have similarly applied the
term.[18] Despite this common judgment about Delibes, his
skill in writing melodies was definitely not his salient
talent. His real strengths were in other areas especially:
a natural ability for devising rhythms for ballet music; a
graceful, charming, elegant, polished, and lively style;
excellent harmonics; a sense of precision and order; and
outstanding orchestrations. This last characteristic was
perhaps his strongest point, as has been touched upon by
various authors. For example, Adam Carse, in his history of
orchestration, feels that Delibes' orchestrations were
exceptional,[19] and Gabriel Pierné and Henry Woollett (in an
essay on the history of orchestration) consider Delibes to
be a delicate orchestrator with fine and ingenious scores.[20]

DELIBES' HISTORICAL ROLE

With Delibes' music as a whole critically praised, and
three of his major works popular with the public, one might
inquire why he isn't one of the leading names in music.
There are two reasons. One, Delibes was not a prolific
composer and despite his overall quality his lower quantity
has decidedly affected his fame. Even the most expansive
view of Delibes' productivity attributes to him only seven
major works, three ballets and four operas. One of the
operas (**Kassya**) was unfinished and one of the ballets (**La**

source) has been emasculated in reputation by being in
reality only a partial ballet. In essence then, he completed only five important compositions. Two, and just as
vital, is the "social status" of his music. He did not
attempt any works of the highest status, that is, symphonies,
concertos, and related pieces. He did write some works of
the next highest status, opera, but his greatest success
there, **Lakmé,** is not one of the very top-ranked operas
(partially because of an inferior plot). Although some
composers established great fame with one opera, notably
Bizet with **Carmen, Lakmé** falls short of being truly
exceptional.

Delibes' most famous and respected works were his
ballets. This was unfortunate for his public image, since
ballet music has generally been treated as a genre of lower
status than symphonic and operatic works.[21] Even Tchaikovsky's great ballets, on which a substantial block of his
renown is based, are sometimes given less emphasis by
historians than his other works. So although Delibes was
the "father of modern ballet-music" and probably strongly
influenced Tchaikovsky, his affinity for a "lesser" genre
combined with a small amount of major works has created a
situation which limits his fame. This has prompted Paul
Landormy, among others, to justly complain that Delibes has
not been accorded the recognition he merits.[22]

The most apt statement of this unfortunate phenomenon,
possibly, is the description of Delibes given in **The Simon
and Schuster Book of the Ballet** as "a composer still
undervalued today."[23] His name is not well-known, but some
of his compositions are. As an indicator of his semi-
anonymity, portions of his music are well established in
American popular culture without general recognition of him.
For example, the pizzicati from the third act of **Sylvia** can
be found in a number of animated cartoons and television
advertisements and an American television program of the
mid-1980's, **Knight Rider,** bases its main musical theme on a
melody from the same act of **Sylvia.** On an international
basis, his music has been used in at least fifteen new
ballets created in at least five countries between the years
1900 and 1981, and this is not counting direct excerpts like
Pas de deux: La source. Yet the usual reaction to his name
in many western nations is: "Who is Delibes?"

Probably the best summation of Delibes' value to the
world's culture was expressed by Edwin Evans. Relating a
conversation with Alexander Glazunov, Evans wrote that he
and Glazunov agreed that "no list of the great masters of

music was complete that did not include the name of
Delibes...Musicians are too prone to consider greatness
a monopoly of those who enrich the more serious forms of
their art, which Delibes did not aspire to do. He was a
great master in the sense that Johann Strauss was a great
master. Moreover, he was a great master of French music."[24]

NOTES

(The numbers refer to the items in the bibliography)

1.   See, for example, items 10, 14, and 41.

2.   For more information on his life and works, see his
     major biographies (items 14 and 16), the better
     essays on him (items 8, 9, 21, 23, 24, 32, 37, 38,
     41, 42, 47, 49, 60, and 61), or the thesis by Margie
     Boston (item 10).

3.   Items 19 and 39.

4.   Items 20, 22, and 53. This monument was erected at
     La Fléche, in Delibes' home region. Another monument
     was erected at the same time in the village where he
     was born.

5.   Items 27, 48, and 57.

6.   Pages 6 and 7.

7.   Items 55, 56, and 95.

8.   Items 55 and 95.

9.   Items 71 and 74.

10.   Items 93, 95, and the item following 92.

11.   Item 95 and the item following 92.

12.   Item 36.

13.   Items 8 and 9.

14.   Item 21.

15.   Item 242.

16.   Item 24.

17.   Item 41.

18.   For example, see item 332.

19.   Item 12.

20.   Item 45.

21.   See item 94.
22.   Item 37.
23.   Item following 176.
24.   Items 72 and 73.

MUSICAL WORKS

BALLETS

(Unless otherwise indicated,
all first performed in Paris)

1. **La source (Naïla)** (3 acts)

    November 12, 1866, Opéra, in collaboration with
    Léon Minkus; scenarists, Charles Nuitter
    [Charles Truinet] and Arthur Saint-Léon;
    Delibes composed scenes 2 and 3, Minkus 1 and 4;
    Delibes' song **Regrets!** was derived from his
    section.

2. **Valse, ou, Pas des fleurs (Naïla Waltz)**

    October 21, 1867, Opéra; divertissement added to
    a revival of Adam's **Le corsaire.**

3. **Coppélia, ou, La fille aux yeux d'émail** (2 acts)

    May 25, 1870, Opéra; scenarists, Charles Niutter
    [Charles Truinet] and Arthur Saint-Léon, after
    E.T.A. Hoffmann; some sources indicate Nuitter to
    be the sole author of the scenario; sometimes the
    date of the first performance is given as May 21.

4. **Sylvia, ou, La nymphe de Diane** (3 acts)

    June 14, 1876, Opéra; scenarists, Jules Barbier
    and Baron Jacques de Reinach, after Torquato
    Tasso's **Aminta**; some sources indicate that Louis
    Mérante also collaborated on the scenario.

5. **Six airs de danse dans le style ancien**

    November 22, 1882, Comédie-Française; dances
    added to a revival of Victor Hugo's **Le roi
    s'amuse.**

OPERATIC WORKS

(Unless otherwise indicated, all
first performed in Paris)

1. **Deux sous de charbon, ou, Le suicide de Bigorneau**
   (1 act asphyxie lyrique/operetta)

February 9, 1856, Folies-Nouvelles; librettist,
Jules Moinaux.

2.   **Deux vielles gardes (Double garde, ou, Un malade que
     se porte bien)** (1 act opérette bouffe/opéra bouffe/
     bouffonerie musical/operetta)

> August 8, 1856, Bouffes-Parisiens; librettists,
> Théodore Ferdinand Vallon de Villeneuve and
> Alphonse Lemonnier.

3.   **Six demoiselles à marier** (1 act opérette bouffe/
     operetta)

> November 12, 1856, Bouffes-Parisiens;
> librettists, E. Jaime and Adolphe Choler.

4.   **Maître Griffard (Monsieur Griffard)** (1 act opéra
     comique/opéra bouffe)

> October 3, 1857, Théâtre-Lyrique; librettists,
> Eugène Mestépès and Adolphe Jaime.

5.   **La fille du golfe** (1 act opéra comique)

> Unperformed work published in 1859; librettist,
> Charles Nuitter [Charles Truinet].

6.   **L'omellete à la Follembuche** (1 act opérette
     bouffe/operetta)

> June 8, 1859, Bouffes-Parisiens; librettists,
> Eugène Labiche and Marc Michel.

7.   **Monsieur de Bonne-Etoile** (1 act operetta/opéra
     comique)

> February 4, 1860, Bouffes-Parisiens; librettist,
> Philippe Gille.

8.   **Les musiciens de l'orchestre** (2 act operetta/opérette
     bouffe)

> January 25, 1861, Bouffes-Parisiens, in collabo-
> ration with Jacques Offenbach, Jules Erlanger,
> and Aristide Hignard; librettists, P.A.A. Pitaud
> de Forges and Achille Bourdois.

9.   **Les eaux d'Ems** (1 act operetta/comédie)

> Summer, 1861, Kursaal d'Ems; librettists, Hector
> Crémieux and Ludovic Halévy.

10. **Mon ami Pierrot** (1 act operetta)

July, 1862, Kursaal d'Ems; librettist, Joseph
Philippe Simon Lockroy.

11. **Le jardinier et son seigneur** (1 act opéra comique)

May 1, 1863, Théâtre-Lyrique; librettists, Michel
Carré and Théodore Barrière.

12. **La tradition** (fantaisie-prologue en vers)

January 5, 1864, Bouffes-Parisiens; librettist,
H. Derville.

13. **Grand nouvelle** (1 act operetta)

Unperformed work published in 1864 [in collaboration with Elisa Adam-Boisgontier?].

14. **Le serpent à plumes** (1 act farce/opéra bouffe/opéra
comique)

December 16, 1864, Bouffes-Parisiens; librettists,
Philippe Gille and Cham [Amédée de Noé].

15. **Le boeuf Apis** (2 act opéra bouffe/opérette bouffe/
operetta)

April 25, 1865, Bouffes-Parisiens; librettists,
Philippe Gille and Eugène Furpille.

16. **Malbrough s'en va-t-en guerre** (4 act opéra bouffe/
grand opérette/opérette bouffe)

December 13, 1867, Athénée, in collaboration with
Georges Bizet, Émile Jonas, and Édouard Legouix;
librettists, William Busnach and Paul Siraudin;
Delibes composed act 4.

17. **L'écossais de Chatou (Montagnards écossais)** (1 act
bouffonnerie/operetta)

January 16, 1869, Bouffes-Parisiens; librettists,
Phillipe Gille and Adolphe Jaime.

18. **La cour du roi Pétaud** (3 act opéra bouffe/operetta)

April 24, 1869, Variétés; librettists, Adolphe
Jaime and Philippe Gille.

19.   **Fleur-de-lys** (1 act opéra bouffe)

> Unperformed work published in 1873;
> librettist, H.B. Farnie.

20.   **Le roi l'a dit** (3 act opéra comique)

> May 24, 1873, Opéra-Comique; librettist, Édmond
> Gondinet.

21.   **Jean de Nivelle** (3 act opera/drame lyrique/opéra
comique)

> March 8, 1880, Opéra-Comique; librettists, Édmond
> Gondinet and Philippe Gille; Gondinet has been
> indicated as the sole author of the libretto.

22.   **Lakmé** (3 act opera/opéra comique)

> April 14, 1883, Opéra-Comique; librettists,
> Édmond Gondinet and Philippe Gille.

23.   **Kassya** (4 act opera/drame lyrique/opéra comique)

> March 24, 1893, Opéra-Comique; librettists,
> Philippe Gille and Henri Meilhac; posthumously
> completed, including most of the orchestration,
> by Jules Massenet; Delibes died before composing
> an overture, and Massenet did not fill this void.

24.   **Le Don Juan suisse** (4 act opéra bouffe)

> Lost.

25.   **La princesse Ravigote** (3 act opéra bouffe)

> Lost.

26.   **Le roi des montagnes** (3 act opéra comique)

> Sketches.

27.   **Jacques Callot**

> Abandoned.

CANTATAS AND LYRIC SCENE

1.   **Alger** (cantata)

> August 15, 1865, Opéra, Paris; lyrics by Joseph
> Méry.

2. **La mort d'Orphée** (lyric scene for tenor solo, chorus, and orchestra)

    July 25, 1878, Trocadéro, Paris.

3. **Cantate Oluber**

    Piano-vocal score published in 1881.

4. **Honneur au frère Garnier** (cantata for narrator and chorus, with piano accompaniment)

    1889, probably Paris.

RELIGIOUS MUSIC

1. **Agnus Dei** (two voices)

    Undated, possibly 1880's or early 1890's.

2. **Ave Maris Stella** (two voices)

    Undated, possibly 1880's or early 1890's.

3. **Ave Verum** (two voices)

    Undated, possibly 1880's or early 1890's.

4. **Messe Brève** (two equal voices, with organ and string quartet accompaniment)

    Undated, possibly 1880's or early 1890's.

5. **O Salutaris** (two and three equal voices)

    Undated, possibly 1880's or early 1890's.

MUSIC FOR PLAYS

(See also the ballet **Six airs de danse
dans le style ancien**)

1. **Le chant des Lavandières (Chanson des Lavandières)** (serenade for solo voice, chorus, and instruments)

    1879; for Victor Hugo's **Ruy Blas,** act 2; a chorus and a song, both under the title **Sérénade du Ruy Blas,** were derived from this.

2. **Ninon, Ninon, que fais-tu de la vie?** (serenade for baritone and mandolin or harp)

    1879; for Alfred de Musset's **À quoi rêvent les**

jeunes filles; a song entitled **Sérénade à Ninon** was derived from this.

3. **Beau chevalier qui partez pour la guerre**

    1882; for Alfred de Musset's **Barberine**; a song entitled **Chanson de Barbarine** was derived from this.

4. Incidental music for Henri Meilhac's **Cynthia**.

    Undated.

CHORUSES

1. **Les dandys parisiens** (4 voices)

    April, 1858?; lyrics by A. Vialon; derived from the chansonette **Le code fashionable**.

2. **La nuit de Noël** (4 male voices)

    June 5, 1859, Lisieux, France; lyrics by Philippe Gille.

3. **Les abeilles** (2 and 3 equal voices, with or without accompaniment)

    1860's or 1870's?, Sceaux, France; lyrics by Henri Murger.

4. **Le dimanche** (2 and 3 equal voices, with or without accompaniment)

    1860's?; lyrics by Henri Murger.

5. **La Marseillaise** (4 male voices)

    1860's?, Opéra, Paris; lyrics by Rouget de l'Isle.

6. **Noël** (3 equal voices, with or without accompaniment)

    1860's?; lyrics by André Bouéry.

7. **Les novégiennes** (2 female voices, with accompaniment)

    1860's?; lyrics by Philippe Gille.

8. **Les nymphes des bois** (2 female voices, with accompaniment)

    1860's?; lyrics by Charles Nuitter [Charles Truinet].

9. **Les pifferari** (3 equal voices, with or without accompaniment)

> 1860's or 1870's, Sceaux, France; lyrics by Philippe Gille.

10. **Hymne de Noël** (4 mixed voices, without accompaniment)

> 1865, Paris.

11. **Pastorale** (4 male voices, without accompaniment)

> 1865, Vincennes, France; lyrics by Camille du Locle.

12. **Avril** (4 mixed voices, without accompaniment)

> 1866, Paris; lyrics by Rémy Belleau; a song of the same name was derived from this.

13. **Les chants lorrains (Chant lorrain)** (4 male voices, without accompaniment)

> 1866, Nancy, France; lyrics by Philippe Gille.

14. **Les lansquenets** (4 male voices, without accompaniment)
> 1866, Boulogne, France; lyrics by Philippe Gille.

15. **Marche des soldats** (4 male voices, without accompaniment)

> 1866, Paris; lyrics by Charles Nuitter [Charles Truinet].

16. **Les prix** (2 equal voices, with accompaniment)
> 1866, Sceaux, France; lyrics by Gustave Chouquet.

17. **Au printemps** (3 equal voices, without accompaniment)
> 1867, Sceaux, France; lyrics by Philippe Gille.

18. **Chant de la Paix** (4 male voices, or 6 mixed voices, or 3 and 4 equal voices, with or without accompaniment)

> 1867, Vincennes, France; lyrics by Louis Girard.

19. **C'est Dieu** (4 mixed voices, without accompaniment)

> 1868, Paris; lyrics by Émile Hinzelin.

20. **La cour des miracles** (4 male voices or 3 and 4 equal

voices, with or without accompaniment)

> 1868, Paris; lyrics by Émile de Lyden.

21. **En avant!** (3 and 4 equal voices)

> 1868, Paris; lyrics by Paul de France.

22. **Le marchand d'oubliés** (2 male voices, with accompaniment)

> 1868; lyrics by Aug. Parmentier.

23. **Trianon** (4 male voices, without accompaniment)

> 1868, Paris; lyrics by Émile de Lyden.

24. **L'echeveau de fil** (3 equal voices, without accompaniment)

> 1874, Sceaux, France; lyrics by Louis Ratisbonne.

25. **Le pommier** (3 equal voices, without accompaniment)

> 1877, Sceaux, France; lyrics by Philippe Gille.

26. **Sérénade de Ruy Blas** (solo and chorus, with accompaniment)

> 1879; lyrics by Victor Hugo; derived from **Le chant des Lavandières,** music originally for a play.

27. **Les trois oiseaux** (2 female voices, with accompaniment)

> 1880's or 1890's?; lyrics by François Coppée.

28. **Voyage enfantin** (3 equal voices, with accompaniment)

> 1884, Paris; lyrics by Philippe Gille.

SONGS

(All are mélodies except for the first four,
which are chansonettes)

1. **La taxe sur la viande**

> 1856; lyrics by Jules Moinaux.

2. **Les animaux de Granville**

> 1856 or 1857; lyrics by A. Vialon.

3. **Les deux moulins**

    1856 or 1857; lyrics by A. Vialon.

4. **Le code fashionable**

    February, 1858?; lyrics by A. Vialon; the chorus
    Les dandys parisiens was derived from this.

5. **Bonjour Suzon!**

    1863; lyrics by Alfred de Musset.

6. **Eglogue**

    1863; lyrics by Victor Hugo.

7. **Avril**

    1866; lyrics by Rémy Belleau; derived from a
    chorus of the same name.

8. **Le meilleur moment des amours**

    1872; lyrics by René Sully-Prudhomme.

9. **Les filles de Cadix (Chanson espagnole)**

    1874; lyrics by Alfred de Musset.

10. **Sérénade à Ninon**

    1879; lyrics by Alfred de Musset; derived from
    Ninon, Ninon, que fais-tu de la vie?, music
    originally for a play.

11. **Sérénade de Ruy Blas**

    1879; lyrics by Victor Hugo; derived from **Le
    chant des Lavandières,** music originally for a
    play.

12. **Chanson hongroise**

    1880; lyrics by François Coppée.

13. **Chanson de Barberine**

    1882; lyrics by Alfred de Musset; derived from
    Beau chevalier que partez pour la guerre, music
    originally for a play.

14. **Vieille chanson**
    1882; lyrics by Victor Hugo, derived from the
    dialogue of his play **Le roi s'amuse.**

15. **Epithalame**
    1888; lyrics by Édouard Grenier.

16. **Chrysanthème**
    1889; lyrics by Paul Fuchs.

17. **À ma mignonne**
    1890; lyrics by J. Renaut.

18. **Faut-il chanter**?
    1891; lyrics by Vte. de Borrelli.

19. **Arioso**
    Undated; lyrics by Armand Silvestre.

20. **Blanche et rose**
    Undated; lyrics by Armand Silvestre.

21. **Chanson de l'oiseleur (Pastorale)**
    Undated; lyrics by Joseph Philippe Simon Lockroy.

22. **Chant de l'aimée**
    Undated; lyrics by Philippe Gille.

23. **Départ**
    Undated; lyrics by Émile Augier.

24. **Heure de soir**
    Undated; lyrics by Armand Silvestre.

25. **Myrto**
    Undated; lyrics by Armand Silvestre.

26. **Peine d'amour**
    Undated; lyrics by Armand Silvestre.

27. **Que l'heure est donc brève**

Undated; lyrics by Armand Silvestre.

28. **Regrets!**

Undated; lyrics by Armand Silvestre; the music was derived from **La source.**

29. **Le rossignol**

Undated; lyrics from an "old poem".

PIANO MUSIC

1. **Echo** (polka for two hands)
1856 or 1857?

2. **Le muletier de Tolède** (polka-mazurka for four hands)
1856 or 1857?

3. **Musette** (polka-mazurka for four hands)
1856 or 1857?

4. **Souvenir d'allemagne—impromptu** (sketch for piano, two hands)
1860; possibly not published.

5. **Intermezzo** (four hands)
1860's or 1870's?

6. **Les lanciers de la garde** (quadrille for four hands)
1860's or 1870's?

7. **Musette écossaise** (two or four hands)
1860's or 1870's?

8. **Une nuit à Séville** (polka for four hands)
1860's or 1870's?

9. **Rigaudon** (two hands)
1860's or 1870's?

10. **Romance hongroise sans paroles** (two hands)
1860's or 1870's?

11. **Souvenir lointain** (two hands)
          1860's or 1870's?

                    MISCELLANEOUS COMPOSITIONS

 1. **Horse-guard's March** (instrumental work)
          1861.

 2. **Morceau** (flute and piano)
          1876.

 3. **Fanfare A, Fanfare B** (instrumental works)
          1889; for the Exposition universelle.

 4. **Monts d'Auvergne: Grand fantaisie pour trompes de chasse en ré** (instrumental work)
          1890?

 5. Minor arrangements, orchestrations, derivatives (at least 7).

                    ARRANGEMENT AND COMPLETION OF
                    THEATRICAL WORKS BY OTHERS

 1. Adam, Adolphe. **À Clichy.**
          Vocal-piano score published in 1855.

 2. Gounod, Charles. **Faust.**
          Vocal-piano score in collaboration with Émile
          Perier, published 1860.

 3. _____ . **Sapho.**
          Vocal-piano score in collaboration with Émile
          Perier, published 1860.

 4. Offenbach, Jacques. **Belle Lurette.**
          Posthumously completed by Delibes and produced
          October 30, 1880.

 5. _____ . **Mamzelle Moucheron.**
          Posthumously completed by Delibes and produced
          May 10, 1881.

6.   Massé, Victor. **La reine topaze**

   Undated arrangement of score.

7.   Semet, Théophile. **Gil-Blas.**

   Undated vocal-piano score.

WORKS DERIVED FROM DELIBES' MUSIC

1. **Ucheniki Diupre (Les élèves de Dupré)** (ballet)

   February 14, 1900 (Julian calendar), Hermitage
   Theater, St. Petersburg; scenarist, Marius
   Petipa; the music was by Delibes and others.

2. **Radha** (ballet)

   January 28, 1906, New York Theatre, New York; the
   music was from **Lakmé.**

3. **Cobras** (ballet)

   March 26, 1906, Hudson Theatre, New York; the
   music was from **Lakmé.**

4. **Karnaval (Le carnaval)** (ballet)

   December 8, 1913 (Julian calendar), Bolshoi
   Theater, Moscow; the music was by Delibes and
   several others.

5. **Pipes of Pan** (ballet)

   April 13, 1914, Kentucky Theatre, Paducah, Kentucky; the music was "arranged from original
   Indian airs" (**Lakmé?**).

6. **Soir de fête (Soirée de fête)** (ballet)

   June 30, 1925, Opéra, Paris; the music was from
   La source.

7. **Stagefright** (ballet)

   March 13, 1927, Little Theatre, New York.

8. **Pique-nique—1860** (ballet)

   December 4th, 1932, Guild Theatre, New York.

9. **Fadetta** (ballet)
   March 21, 1934, Kirov Theater, Leningrad;

scenarists, Leonid Lavrovski and V. Solov'ev;
the music was from **Sylvia** and other sources.

10.   **Fluorescences** (ballet)

February 9, 1938, Palais Garnier, Paris; the
music was by Delibes and five others; Delibes'
section of the music was called "Fleurs", and
may have been **Valse, ou, Pas des fleurs.**

11.   **Pièce d'occasion** (ballet)

September 10, 1959, Festival Hall, London; the
music was from **La source.**

12.   **Pas de Deux and Divertissement** (ballet)

January 14, 1965, State Theater, New York; the
music was from **La source, Sylvia,** and **Valse, ou,
Pas des fleurs.**

13.   **Celebration** (ballet)

June 29, 1973, Teatro Nuovo, Spoleto, Italy; ten
pas de deux (including the pas de deux from
Coppélia), plus a prologue and epilogue.

14.   **Le jardin animé** (ballet)

May 20, 1981, Metropolitan Opera House, New York;
the music was by Delibes, Adolphe Adam, and
Riccardo Drigo; the music by Delibes included
Valse, ou, Pas des fleurs.

15.   **Don Parasol** (ballet)

September or October, 1981, Komische Oper,
Berlin; scenarist, Paul Taglioni revised by Bernd
Köllinger; this was a revival of an 1868 ballet,
with the original music by Peter Hertel replaced
by music from the second act of **La source** and
from **Sylvia.**

WORKS POSSIBLY AFFILIATED WITH DELIBES

1.   **Les brigands** (1875 ballet by Léon Minkus).

2.   **Les aventures de Pelée** (1876 ballet by Léon Minkus).

3.   **La rose et le papillon** (ballet by Aleksandr Gorski).

4.   **Tennis** (ballet by Michel Fokine).

BIBLIOGRAPHY

DELIBES' WRITINGS

1. Delibes, Léo. **Discours prononcé à l'inauguration de la statue élevée à la memoire de Victor Massé à Lorient.** Paris: Didot, 1887.

   Speech given on the occasion of the dedication of a memorial statue to Victor Massé.

2. ———. "Mesdames de la halle." **Le gaulois hebdomadaire** 16 (March 6, 1858): 4.

   Review of Jacques Offenbach's work. Delibes used the pseudonym "Eloi Delbès" on this occasion and for another review (item 4).

3. ———. **Notice sur Victor Massé lue à l'Académie des beaux-arts le 21 novembre 1885.** Paris: Didot, 1885.

   Memorial essay on Victor Massé.

4. ———. "Reprise de la Perle du Brésil." **Le gaulois hebdomadaire** 16 (March 13, 1858): 2.

   Review of Felicien David's work.

GENERAL WORKS ON DELIBES

5. Albrecht, Otto E. **A Census of Autograph Music Manuscripts of European Composers in American Libraries.** Philadelphia: University of Pennsylvania Press, 1953, pp. 101-07.
   ML 135.A2 A4

   Forty-eight items of Delibes' are given on this list of composer's manuscripts in United States libraries. Description and location of each item are provided.

6. Baldwin, Lillian. **A Listener's Anthology of Music.** New York: Silver Burdett, 1948, vol. 2, pp. 401-03. Citation also used following item 241.
   MT 90.B25

Very good general information on Delibes, particularly on his personal characteristics and on his
ballet music.

7.   Bellaigue, Camille. **L'année musicale.** Paris:
     Delagrave, 1889.

Has some valuable contemporary material on Delibes,
including a very good extended personal description
which among other things portrays him as being like
"a well-fed American and good-natured child". (Items
10 and 14 also contain this description.)

8.   Boschot, Adolphe. **La musique et la vie.** Paris:
     Plon, 1931, pp. 96-102.
     ML 60.B786 M7

Very readable essay on the life and works of
Delibes, with some good material about Delibes' per-
sonality. One of his main themes is "the return of
Delibes", that is, Delibes' regaining public favor.
The author admires Delibes very much, entitling the
essay "Léo Delibes, ou, L'heureuse destinée" (Delibes'
Happy Destiny).

9.   ———— . **Portraits de musiciens.** Paris: Plon,
     1947-, vol. 2, pp. 69-74.
     ML 385.B8

Same basic essay as item 8.

10. Boston, Margie Viola. "An Essay on the Life and Works
     of Leo Delibes." Doctor of Musical Arts Diss.,
     University of Iowa, 1981. Citation also used fol-
     lowing items 105, 300, 306, and 347.

Best and most sizeable English-language work on
Delibes (96 leaves). It is based primarily on the two
biographies of the composer (items 14 and 16). In
addition to a general history and description of
Delibes' life and works, the thesis contains some very
good material on his personal characteristics, the
most comprehensive and valuable list of his works, the
best bibliography to date, plus good histories of **Jean
de Nivelle, Lakmé,** and **Kassya,** and synopses of **La
source, Jean de Nivelle,** and **Kassya.** The dissertation was also issued by University Microfilms, Ann
Arbor.

11. Bruneau, Alfred. **La musique française: Rapport sur**

musique en France du XIIIe au XXe siècle...
Paris: E. Fasquelle, 1901, pp. 103–05.
ML 270.4.B89

Presents some very favorable opinion on Delibes
ten years after his death. This is a report on the
state of French music as of 1901.

12. Carse, Adam. **The History of Orchestration.** New York:
     Dover, 1964, pp. 299–300.
     ML 455.C32 1964   ISBN 0486212580

     Excellent treatment of Delibes' orchestrations,
     which, the author feels, were very skilled. Another
     edition was published in 1925 by Kegan Paul.

13. Chamfray, Claude. "Léo Delibes." **Le courrier
     musical de France** 41 (1973): 37–38.

     Very handy chronology of Delibes, focusing on his
     more historically or artistically important works.
     There is one glaring error. Delibes' professor of
     composition in 1848 is indicated as "Paul Adam" in-
     stead of "Adolphe Adam".

14. Coquis, André. **Léo Delibes: Sa vie et son oeuvre
     (1836–1891).** Paris: Richard-Masse, 1957. 166 p.

     Comprehensive treatise on Delibes' life and works,
     but smaller and somewhat less useful than the biog-
     raphy by Henri de Curzon (item 16). The survey of
     Delibes' works is very good, including some musical
     themes. There is also much interesting data on his
     personal life and characteristics. Perhaps the best
     description of Delibes, by Camille Bellaigue, is
     quoted. (The description is also found in items 7 and
     10.) In addition, a good list of works and satisfac-
     tory bibliography is included, plus a photograph of
     the house where Delibes was born. Overall, this is
     better than Cruzon in coverage of Delibes' personal
     life, but not as strong as Curzon in coverage of
     Delibes' works.

15. Curtiss, Mina. **Bizet and His World.** New York: Knopf,
     1958. Citation also used following item 275.
     ML 410.B62 C87

     Contains a fair amount of material about Delibes'
     relationship/interface with his colleague Bizet.
     Other biographies of Bizet usually have some material

on Delibes. Editions were also published in London
(1959) and in Geneva (1962).

16.   Curzon, Henri de. **Léo Delibes: Sa vie et ses oeuvres
      (1836–1892).** Paris: G. Legouix, 1926. 223 p.
      ML 410.D343 C8

      Most comprehensive and valuable treatise on
      Delibes' life and works, well organized and very
      readable. Almost all of Delibes' works, even minor
      ones, receive some coverage, with **La source, Coppélia,
      Le roi l'a dit, Jean de Nivelle, Sylvia, Lakmé,** and
      Kassya receiving significant attention. This is
      superior to Coquis (item 14) in the treatment of
      Delibes' works, but Coquis provides more personal data.
      One of this book's best features is a rare photo-
      graphed portrait. Unfortunately, there is no bibli-
      ography or list of works.

17.   Dayrolles, Albert. "La classe de Léo Delibes au Con-
      servatoire." **Ménestrel** 91 (1929): 317–19.

      Essay on Delibes' professorship at the Paris
      Conservatory.

18.   ———— . "Léo Delibes". **Revue du monde musical et
      dramatique** 6 (April 21, 1883): 241–43.

      Contemporary article on Delibes.

19.   Delaborde, Henri. **Discours prononcé au nom du
      l'Académie des beaux-arts aux funérailles de Léo
      Délibes, le 19 janvier 1891.** Paris: Didot, 1891.

      Oration at Delibes' funeral. Item 39 is another
      funeral oration.

20.   Dorchain, Auguste. **Chant pour Léo Delibes, dis aux
      fêtes d'inauguration de son monument à La Flèche,
      le 18 juin 1899.** Paris: A. Lemerre, 1899.

      Speech given at the dedication of a monument to
      Delibes in his home region. Items 22 and 53 also are
      speeches on that occasion.

21.   Downes, Olin. **The Lure of Music: Depicting the Human
      Side of Great Composers with Stories of Their In-
      spired Creations.** New York: Harper, 1918,
      pp.101–06.
      MT 150.D69

Well written and very colorful general essay on
Delibes, and quite complimentary to Delibes' music.
Among the comments are "master of delicious ballet
music," and "to Delibes the ballet was not a series
of hackneyed evolutions, but a poem, a dream of most
delicate beauty."

22. DuBois, Théodore. "Discours prononcé aux fêtes
     d'inauguration du monument élevé à la memoire de
     Léo Delibes, à La Fleche, le 18 juin 1889." **Le
     ménestrel** (June 25, 1899).

     Speech given at the dedication of a monument to
     Delibes in his home region. Items 20 and 53 also are
     speeches on that occasion.

23. Ewen, David. **Great Composers, 1300–1900: A Bio-
     graphical and Critical Guide.** New York: H.W.
     Wilson, 1966, pp. 107–09.
     ML 105.E944

     Well-done general reference article very favorable
     to Delibes, with several interesting and valuable
     quotes.

24. ———— . **The Lighter Classics in Music: A
     Comprehensive Guide to Musical Masterworks in a
     Lighter Vein by 187 Composers.** New York: Arco,
     1961, pp. 68–71.
     MT 6.E9

     Very good general essay on Delibes which describes
     his music in very positive terms, referring to the
     elegance of Delibes' style and his warm lyricism,
     richness of harmonics and rhythm, and delicacy of
     orchestration.

25. Fétis, François Joseph. **Biographie universelle des
     musiciens et bibliographie général de la musique:
     Supplément et complément.** Edited by Arthur Pougin.
     Paris: Didot, 1878–1880, vol. 1, pp. 251–53.
     ML 105.F422

     Good contemporary reference article. There were
     other editions.

26. ———— . **Biographie universelle des musicians et
     bibliographie général de la musique: Supplément et
     complément.** Edited by Arthur Pougin. Brussels:
     Culture et civilization, 1963, vol. 1, pp. 251–53.

ML 105.F422 1963

Reprint of item 15.

27. Guiraud, Ernest. **Notice sur la vie et les oeuvres de
      Léo Delibes.** Paris: Didot, 1892.

    Memorial essay presented to the Académie des beaux-
    arts on April 2, 1892.

28. Harding, James. **Jacques Offenbach: A Biography.**
      London: J. Calder, 1980.
    ML 410.041 H37   ISBN 0714538353

    Has miscellaneous material on the relationship/
    interface between Offenbach and Delibes. Other biog-
    raphies of Offenbach usually have some material on
    Delibes.

29. _____ . **Massenet.** London: Dent, 1970. Citation
      also used following item 347.
    ML 410.M41 H4   ISBN 0460039288

    Has some material on Delibes' relationship/interface
    with his friend Massenet, including Massenet's com-
    pletion of **Kassya.**

30. "In Memoriam, Leo Delibes." **Musica** 15 (February
      1961): 96.

    Brief essay commemorating the 125th anniversary of
    Delibes' birth. This is a good example of recent
    German commentary on Delibes.

31. Jullien, Adolphe, and Alfred Loewenberg. "Delibes,
      (Clément Philibert) Léo." **Grove's Dictionary of
      Music and Musicians.** 5th ed. Edited by Eric Blom.
      New York: St. Martin's, 1954-61, vol. 2,
      pp. 650-51.
    ML 100.G885 1954

    Good general reference article reflecting opinion
    of a generation ago.

32. Kirstein, Lincoln. "Léo Delibes and the Inscape of
      Coppelia." **Dance and Dancers** 26 (March 1975):
      28-29, 38. Citation also used following item 158.

    Excellent essay, very favorable to Delibes, on
    Coppélia and its composer.

33. Labat-Poussin, Bridgette, ed. **Archives du Théâtre
      national de l'Opéra: AJ13 1 à 1466: Inventaire.**

Paris: Archives nationales, 1977.
ML 136.P2 058   ISBN 286000016X

Inventory of the archives of the Paris Opéra, containing 7 citations for Delibes. The indexes are excellent.

34. Lajarte, Théodore de, ed. **Bibliothèque musicale du Théâtre de l'Opéra: Catalogue historique, chronologique, anecdotique.** 2 vols. Paris: Librairie des bibliophiles, 1878.
ML 136.P2 06

Presents the repertory of the Paris Opéra from 1671 to 1876, including material on Delibes' works.

35. ———— . **Bibliothèque musicale du Théâtre de l'Opéra: Catalogue historique, chronologique, anecdotique.** 2 vols. Hildesheim: G. Olms, 1969.

Reprint of item 34.

36. Lalo, Pierre. **De Rameau à Ravel: Portraits et Souvenirs.** Paris: A. Michel, 1947, pp. 102–08.
ML 385.L35

Interesting general essay, with the sentiment that "great artist" is a somewhat absurd term to describe Delibes, but on the other hand Delibes is a charming musician with fine, lively works and that he is always a good and true French musician.

37. Landormy, Paul. **La musique française de Franck à Debussy.** Paris: Gallimard, 1943, pp. 133–36.
ML 270.4.L265

Good general essay stating that perhaps Delibes has not been given the recognition he merits.

38. Landormy, Paul, and Joseph Loisel. "Léo Delibes." **Encyclopedie de la musique et dictionnaire du Conservatoire.** Edited by Albert Lavignac and Lionel de la Laurencie. Paris: C. Delagrave, 1913–31, pt. 2, vol. 6, pp. 3514–16.
ML 100.E5

Good standard French reference article, over half of which is dedicated to two lists: an excellent catalog of Delibes' works; and one of the best bibliographies on Delibes.

39.   Larraumet, Gustave. **Discours prononcé au nom du**
      Ministre de l'instruction publique et des beaux-
      arts aux funérailles de Léo Delibes, le 19 janvier
      1891. Paris: Imprimerie nationals, 1891.

      Oration at Delibes' funeral. Item 19 is another
      funeral oration.

40.   LeSenne, Camille. "Léo Delibes." **Encyclopedie de la**
      musique et dictionnaire du Conservatoire. Edited
      by Albert Lavignac and Lionel de la Laurencie.
      Paris: C. Delagrave, 1913-31, pt. 1, vol. 3,
      pp. 1763-65.
      ML 100.E5

      Good standard French reference article. There is
      no bibliography nor list of works, but another article
      in the same work (item 38) has both.

41.   Macdonald, Hugh. "Delibes, (Clément Philibert) Léo."
      The New Grove Dictionary of Music and Musicians.
      Edited by Stanley Sadie. London: Macmillan, 1980,
      vol. 5, pp. 336-37.
      ML 100.N48   ISBN 0333231112

      One of the best reference articles on Delibes,
      with an excellent list of his works. The author de-
      scribes Delibes' music very positively, stating that
      Delibes' "workmanship was of the highest order; he
      had a natural gift for harmonic dexterity and a sure
      sense of orchestral colour, and nothing in his music
      is out of place. He was a disciplined composer..."

42.   Marechal, Henri. **Paris, souvenirs d'un musicien.**
      Paris: Hachette, 1907, pp. 33-42.
      ML 410.M324

      Very readable essay, quite supportive of Delibes'
      music, by a contemporary of Delibes.

43.   Noël, Édouard, and Édmond Steullig, eds. **Les annales**
      du théâtre et de la musique. Paris: Charpentier
      [etc.], 1876-95.

      Several years of this publication have contemporary
      material on Delibes.

44.   Parent, D. "Delibes (Clément-Philibert-Léo)." **Dic-**
      tionnaire de biographie française. Edited by J.
      Balteau and others. Paris: Librairie Letouzey et

ané, 1933-, vol. 10, pp. 829-30.
CT 143.D5

Standard French reference article.

45. Pierné, Gabriel, and Henry Woollett. "Ernest Reyer
(1823-1909), Edouard Lalo (1823-1892), Léo Delibes
(1836-1891)" **Encyclopedie de la musique et dictionnaire du conservatoire.** Edited by Albert
Lavignac and Lionel de la Laurencie. Paris: C.
Delagrave, 1913-31, pt. 2, v. 4, pp. 2563-64.
ML 100.E5

In a section on the history of orchestration, gives
a brief but perceptive analysis of Delibes' orchestrations, with an example from **Lakmé.** Delibes is
described as a delicate orchestrator with fine and
ingenious scores.

46. Pierre, Constant, ed. **Le Conservatoire national de
musique et de déclamation: Documents historiques et
administratifs.** Paris: Imprimerie nationale, 1900.
MT 5.P2 C647

Documents of the Paris Conservatory containing some
material on Delibes.

47. Poueigh, Jean [Octave Séré, pseud.]. **Musiciens
français d'aujourd'hui.** 8th ed. Paris: Mercure
de France, 1921, pp. 149-62. Citation also used
following item 110.

Good general essay with a very good bibliography
and a sample of a manuscript from **La source.**

48. Pougin, Arthur. "Léo Delibes, avec portrait, auto-
graphes et liste de ses oeuvres." **Revue encyclo-
pédique,** no. 6 (March 1, 1891): 174-76.

Bibliographical essay on the occasion of Delibes'
death.

49. ———. **Musiciens du XIXe siècle.** Paris:
Fischbacher, 1911, pp. 253-76.
ML 390.P79

Good biographical essay by a contemporary, including the facsimile of a letter from Delibes to
Pougin.

50. Prod'homme, Jacques Gabriel. **L'Opéra, 1699-1925.**

Paris: Delagrave, 1925.
ML 1717.8.P2 P8

History of the Paris Opéra, including the chrono-
logical record of its repertory. There is some data
on Delibes' works.

51.   "Quelques letters inédites: Emmanuel Chabrier, Léo
         Delibes," La revue musicale (1905): 499-501.

Four letters from Chabrier to Delibes, one from
Delibes to Chabrier. Only one has the year indicated
(1886). A reprint of the entire periodical was published in 1968 by A. Schnase, Scarsdale, N.Y.

52.   Rohozinski, Ladislas, ed. Cinquante ans de musique
         française, de 1874 à 1925. 2 vols. Paris:
         Librairie de France, 1925. Citation also used
         following items 238, 334, and 349.

Contains much good material on Delibes, including
a caricature of Delibes on page 40 of volume 1. This
is an excellent collection of essays on French music
of the period, substantial in size, with good illustrations and much detail.

53.   Roujon, Henry. "Discours Prononcé aux fêtes d'inaugu-
         rations du monument élevé à la memoire de Léo
         Delibes, à La Fleche, le 18 juin 1899." Le
         ménestrel (June 25, 1899).

Speech given at the dedication of a monument to
Delibes in his home region. Items 20 and 22 also are
speeches on that occasion.

54.   Sharp, Stuart Walter. "The Twilight of French Opéra
         Lyrique, 1880-1900." Doctor of Musical Arts Diss.,
         University of Kentucky, 1975, leaves 162-222.
         Citation also used following item 334.

Although this section of the dissertation is mostly
an extended musical study of Lakmé, it is also quite
useful for a general understanding of Delibes' music.
The dissertation was also issued by University Microfilms, Ann Arbor.

55.   Studwell, William E. Chaikovskii, Delibes, Stra-
         vinskii: Four Essays on Three Masters. Chicago:
         Prophet Press, 1977, pp. 5-21. Citation also used
         used following item 92.

ML 390.S954

Study of the personal relationship of Delibes and Tchaikovsky, including the Russian's extremely high opinion of the Frenchman (documented by eight letters) and the apparently unsatisfying meeting of the two in Paris in 1886. This and item 95 contain the only extended material on the personal relationship of the two composers.

56.   Tchaikovsky, Peter Il'ich. **The Diaries of Tchaikovsky.** Translated from the Russian, with notes, by Wladimir Lakond. New York: Norton, 1945, p. 87.
ML 410.C4 A22

Tchaikovsky's diary entries for June 20 and 21, 1866, which give his reaction to his only meeting with Delibes (on the 21st). Exposition and analysis of this data is given in items 55 and 95.

57.   Thomé, Francis. "Léo Delibes." **La revue de famille** (February 1891): 265–78.

Memorial essay on Delibes.

58.   Tiersot, Julien. **Un demi-siècle de musique française: Entre les deux guerres, 1870–1917.** Paris: F. Alcan, 1918, pp. 69–71, 177–78.
ML 270.4.T43

Pages 69–71 are a general essay on Delibes, and pages 177–178 are on Delibes teaching at the Paris Conservatory. Another edition, revised, was published in 1924.

59.   Turner, J. Righbie. "Nineteenth-century Autograph Music Manuscripts in the Pierpont Morgan Library." **Nineteenth Century Music** 4, no. 1 (1980): 65.

Contains information on five of Delibes' manuscripts.

60.   Van Vechten, Carl. "Back to Delibes." **Musical Quarterly** 8 (October 1922): 605–10.

Highly recommended general essay on Delibes, emphasizing his contributions to ballet music. If only one essay on Delibes is to be read, this is it.

61.   _____ . "Léo Delibes." **Dance Index** 1 (September–

November 1942): 182–86.

Same essay as item 60.

62.   Waleffe, Pierre. **La vie des grands musiciens**
      français. Paris: Editions du Sud, 1960, p. 215.
      ML 390.W15 V5

      Unusual short essay stressing Delibes' "modest
      origins" and his repudiation of his "humble
      beginnings" after he achieved fame. The author feels
      it is unfortunate that Delibes developed such an atti-
      tude, particularly since he was overall "not such a
      bad fellow."

63.   Wirth, Herman. "Delibes, Léo." **Die Musik in**
      Geschichte und Gegenwart: Allgemeine Enzyklopädie
      der Musik. Edited by Friedrich Blume. Kassel:
      Bärenreiter-Verlag, 1949–79.

      German language reference article.

                    DELIBES' BALLETS IN GENERAL

64.   Arvey, Verna. **Choreographic Music: Music for the**
      Dance. New York: Dutton, 1941, pp. 91–93, 117,
      174, 328.
      ML 3400.A78

      Miscellaneous good material on Delibes' ballets in
      one of the better books on dance music.

65.   Chujoy, Anatole, and Phyllis Winifred Manchester, eds.
      The Dance Encyclopedia. Rev. and enlarged ed.
      New York: Simon and Schuster, 1967.
      GV 1585.C5 1967

      This comprehensive reference book on dance has
      essays on Delibes and his ballets. Another edition
      was published in 1949 by A.S. Barnes, New York.

66.   Clarke, Mary, and Clement Crisp. **Design for Ballet.**
      London: Studio Vista, 1978.
      GV 1782.C56   ISBN 0289705967

      Excellent monograph on design of ballet sets and
      costumes, with some material on Delibes' ballets.
      Another edition was published in 1978 by Hawthorne
      Books, New York.

67.   Clarke, Mary, and David Vaughan, eds. **The Encyclo-
        pedia of Dance & Ballet.** London: Pitman, 1977.
        GV 1585.E53   ISBN 0273010883

      This comprehensive reference book on dance has
essays on Delibes and his ballets. Another edition
was published in 1977 by Putnam, New York.

68.   Cooper, Martin. **French Music from the Death of
        Berlioz to the Death of Fauré.** London: Oxford
        University Press, 1962, pp. 32-33.
        ML 270.4.C7 1961

      Brief but very well written section on Delibes'
ballet music, describing his special talents and affinity for ballet. Another edition was published in
1951.

69.   Davidson, I. "Balety Deliba." **Sovetskaia muzyka** 25
        (February 1961): 79-83.

      One of the better essays on Delibes' ballets,
putting his ballet music in its historical context and
indicating that Delibes felt that a new type of ballet
production must be developed. Item 70 is the English
translation.

70.   ———— . "Leo Delibes' Ballets." **Music Journal** 20
        (January 1962): 87-89, 116.

      Translation of item 69.

71.   Evans, Edwin. "The Ballets." **The Music of
        Tchaikovsky.** Edited by Gerald Abraham. New York:
        Norton, 1946, p. 185.
        ML 410.C4 A5 1946

      Claims that Tchaikovsky's ballets were not influ-
enced by Delibes', as often as has been said. The
citation following item 92 refutes this reasonably
well. Another edition was published in 1969 by
Kennikat Press.

72.   ———— . "The Composer of Coppelia." **Dancing Times,**
        no. 352 (January 1940): 208-09.

      Relates a conversation with Alexander Glazunov in
which both agreed that Delibes "was a great master in
the sense that Johann Strauss was a great master.
Moreover, he was a great master of French music."

73.   _____ . **Music and the Dance, for Lovers of the
       Ballet.** London: H. Jenkins, 1948, pp. 119–21.
       ML 3460.E9

       Same basic essay as item 72.

74.   Garden, Edward. **Tchaikovsky.** London: Dent, 1973,
       p. 65.
       ML 410.C4 G36

       Claims that Tchaikovsky's ballets were not influ-
       enced by Delibes', as has often been said. The cita-
       tion following item 92 refutes this reasonably well.

75.   Guest, Ivor. **Le ballet de l'Opéra de Paris: Trois
       siècles d'histoire et de tradition.** Translation
       by Paul Alexandre. Paris: Théâtre national de
       l'Opéra, 1976.
       GV 1787.G8

       Excellent history on the Paris Opéra's presentation
       of ballets, including **La source, Coppélia, Sylvia**, and
       Soir de fête.

76.   Hanslick, Eduard. **Musikalische Stationen.** Berlin:
       Allg. Verein für Deutsche Literatur, 1885, pp. 96–
       105.

       Contemporary commentary on Delibes' ballets. There
       were other editions.

77.   Haskell, Arnold L., ed. **The Ballet Annual: A Record
       and Yearbook of the Ballet.** London: Black, 1947–
       63.

       Eighteen very good annuals, some published by Mac-
       millan, New York. The last four issues were also by
       Mary Clarke. Some valuable material on Delibes'
       ballets is included.

78.   Koegler, Horst. **The Concise Oxford Dictionary of
       Ballet.** 2d ed. London: Oxford University Press,
       1982.
       GV 1585.K613 1982   ISBN 0193113252

       This comprehensive reference book has articles on
       Delibes and his ballets. Another edition was pub-
       lished in 1977.

79.   Leslie, Serge. **A Bibliography of the Dance Collection
       of Doris Niles & Serge Leslie.** Edited by Cyril

Beaumont. 2 vols. London: C.W. Beaumont, 1966–68.
Z 7514.D2 L4   ISBN 0903102560

Excellent annotated dance bibliography which contains a number of items about Delibes.

80. Lifar, Serge. **La musique par la danse, de Lulli à Prokofiev.** Paris: R. Laffont, 1955, pp. 113–27.
ML 3460.L5

Essay very favorable to Delibes' ballet music, with some material on his relationship to Adam, Tchaikovsky, and others.

81. Miguel, Parmenia. **The Ballerinas from the Court of Louis XIV to Pavlova.** New York: Macmillan, 1972.
GV 1785.A1 M47

Biographies of famous ballerinas, with background historical material. **La source, Coppélia,** and **Sylvia** are covered, especially on pages 239–242.

82. New York Public Library. **Dictionary Catalog of the Dance Collection.** 10 vols. Boston: G.K. Hall, 1974.
Z 7514.D2 N462 1974   ISBN 0816111243

Huge, very well annotated catalog of dance material. It would be difficult to exaggerate the value of this work for ballet research. All types of materials are included: books, articles, audio–visual material, clippings, etc. Films, recordings and other nonprint materials are especially well represented in quantity and in detail. A wealth of historical data is provided. And all of the information is well coordinated by cross references. In the case of Delibes, there is a large amount of useful and accurate information, including data on ballets derived from Delibes' music. Many of the older and rarer items in this bibliography are listed in the catalog, including some items not found elsewhere.

83. ———— . **Bibliographic Guide to Dance.** Boston: G.K. Hall, 1976–.
Z 7514.D2 N462a   ISSN 0360-2737

Yearly supplements (one or two volumes each year) to item 82, with the same exceptional value for research as the main set. 1975 is the first year covered.

84.   Nussbaum, Joseph. **The Fountain: Fox-Trot Ballet.**
       New York: Kayen Music Corp., 1926.

       Jazz ballet adapted from music by Delibes. A later
       version (item 85) is called **Fountainette.**

85.   ———— . **Fountainette.** Cleveland: S. Fox, 1928.

       Jazz ballet adapted from music by Delibes. An
       earlier version (item 84) is called **The Fountain.**

86.   Reyna, Ferdinando. **A Concise History of Ballet.**
       New York: Grosset & Dunlap, 1965.
       GV 1787.R413

       Translation of item 87.

87.   ———— . **Histoire du ballet.** Paris: Éditions
       A. Somogy, 1964.
       GV 1787.R42

       General history of ballet with some material on
       Delibes' ballets.

88.   ———— . **Historia del ballet.** Madrid: Ediciones
       Daimon, Manuel Tamayo, 1965.

       Translation of item 87.

89.   Roslavleva, Natal'ia Petrovna. **Era of the Russian
       Ballet.** New York: Dutton, 1966.
       GV 1787.R675

       History of ballet in Russia, with some information
       on Delibes' ballets. Another edition was published in
       1966 by Gollancz, London.

90.   Searle, Humphrey. **Ballet Music: An Introduction.**
       London: Cassell, 1958, pp. 59-67.
       ML 3460.S4

       Well-written, thoughtful essay on Delibes' ballet
       music, with a high opinion of Delibes. Another
       edition was published in 1973.

91.   ———— . "The Grand Romantic Ballets." **Perspectives
       in Music.** Edited by Leroy Ostransky. Englewood
       Cliffs, N.J.: Prentice-Hall, 1963, pp. 267-72.
       ML 90.075

       Same basic essay as item 90.

92.   Smakov, Gennady. **The Great Russian Dancers.** New
         York: Knopf, 1984.
         GV 1785.A1 S62 1984   ISBN 0294510747

         Biographies of a number of Russian dancers, with
    material on performance of **La source, Coppélia,** and
    Sylvia.

*   Studwell, William E. **Chaikovskii, Delibes,
         Stravinskii,** pp. 22-41. Cited above as item 55.

         Offers strong but not definitive evidence that
    Tchaikovsky modelled his ballets on Delibes'. His-
    torical and logical evidence is used, plus the
    opinions of George Balanchine, Cyril Beaumont, John
    Warrack, David Ewen, Herbert Weinstock, and others.
    This and item 95 are the only known essays that deal
    with the controversy in detail, although short
    passages giving the opposing viewpoint can be found in
    items 71 and 74.

93.   ——— . "The Choreographic Chain: Seventy Years of
         Ballet Music." **Dance Scope** 10 (Spring/Summer
         1976): 51-55.

         Explores the historical connection between the
    ballet music of Adam, Delibes, Tchaikovsky, and Stra-
    vinsky, showing probable direct connections between
    Adam and Delibes, Delibes and Tchaikovsky, and Tchai-
    kovsky and Stravinsky.

94.   ——— . "The Closet Composers: A Heretical View of
         Ballet Music." **Ballet Review** 11 (Summer 1983):
         6, 8.

         Proposes that the reason for the large amount of
    ballet music in non-ballets is the composers' view of
    ballet music as inferior, and also indicates that
    Delibes probably regarded ballet music as inferior to
    other genres.

95.   ——— . "Delibes and Chaikovskii: The Origins of
         Modern Ballet Music." Typescript, 1974.

         Essay (57 leaves) on the ballets of Delibes and
    Tchaikovsky and the personal and artistic relation-
    ships of the two composers. Some of it was published
    in items 55, 93, and 94 and the citation following
    item 92.

96. Swift, Mary Grace. **The Art of the Dance in the
    U.S.S.R.** Notre Dame, Ind.: University of Notre
    Dame Press, 1968.
    GV 1663.S87

    Contains some material on Delibes' ballets as
    presented in the Soviet Union.

97. Swinson, Cyril. **Guidebook to the Ballet.** New York:
    Macmillan, 1961.
    GV 1787.S9   1961

    General book on ballet with some information on
    Delibes' ballets. Another edition was published in
    1960 by English Universities Press, London.

98. Terry, Walter. **The Ballet Companion: A Popular Guide
    for the Ballet-Goer.** New York: Dodd, Mead, 1968.
    GV 1787.T323

    Contains a relatively small amount of material on
    Delibes' ballets, but is very well done.

99. Van Praagh, Peggy, and Peter Brinson. **The Choreo-
    graphic Art.** New York: Knopf, 1963.
    GV 1782.V3   1963

    This good treatise on choreography has some
    material on Delibes' ballets, including brief histories
    of **Coppélia** on page 351 and of **Sylvia** on page 369.
    Another edition was published in 1963 by Black,
    London.

100. Willis, John. **Dance World.** New York: Crown, 1966–
     79.
     GV 1580.D335   ISSN 0070-2692

     Annual on the dance, with miscellaneous data on
     Delibes' ballets.

101. Wilson, George Buckley Laird. **A Dictionary of Ballet.**
     3d ed. New York: Theatre Arts Books, 1974.
     GV 1585.W5   1974   ISBN 0878300392

     General reference book on ballet with some material
     on Delibes and his ballets. Other editions were pub-
     lished in 1961 by Cassell, London, and in 1957 by
     Penguin Books, Harmondsworth.

INDIVIDUAL BALLETS

LA SOURCE

(See also **Soir de fête, Pièce d'occasion, Pas de Deux and Divertissement,** and **Don Parasol**)

1. History, plots, other general works

102. Balanchine, George, and Francis Mason. **Balanchine's Complete Stories of the Great Ballets.** Rev. and enlarged ed. Garden City, N.Y.: Doubleday, 1977, pp. 569-70. Citation also used following items 125, 226, and 263.
     MT 95.B3 1977   ISBN 0385113811

     History and plot.

103. Barnes, Patricia. "New York City Ballet at the State Theater, Lincoln Centre: La Source." **Dance and Dancers** 20 (January 1969): 46.

     On the premiere performance of Balanchine's **Pas de deux: La source.**

104. Beaumont, Cyril W. **Complete Book of Ballets: A Guide to the Principal Ballets of the Nineteenth and Twentieth Centuries.** London: Putnam, 1937, pp. 423-39. Citation also used following items 127 and 227.
     GV 1787.B35

     History and plot. In addition to item 105 below, other editions were published in 1938 by Putnam, New York, and in 1956 by Putnam, London.

105. ———— . **Complete Book of Ballets: A Guide to the Principal Ballets of the Nineteenth and Twentieth Centuries.** Garden City, N.Y.: Garden City Publishing Co., 1941, pp. 354-59. Citation also used following items 127 and 227.
     MT 95.B4 1941

     History and plot.

*   Boston, Margie Viola. "An Essay on the Life and Works of Leo Delibes," leaf 78. Cited above as item 10.
     Plot.

106. Brillant, Maurice. "Du romaticisme à Jacques Rouché." **L'art du ballet des origines à nos jours.**

Paris: Editions du tambourinaire, 1952, pp. 74–75.
Citation also used following items 132 and 227.

On the history of **La source.**

107. Drew, David, ed. **The Decca Book of Ballet.** London:
      F. Muller, 1958, pp. 126–29. Citation also used
      following items 144 and 231.
      MT 95.D74

      History, plot, and musical themes.

108. Dunn, Thomas D. "Delibes and La Source: Some Manu-
      scripts and Documents." **Dance Chronicle** 4, no. 1
      (1981): 1–13. Citation also used following item
      120.

      Excellent scholarly essay on the music of **La
      source,** including its composition, the subsequent
      history of the music, and the confusion between the
      1867 **Pas des fleurs** divertissement (**Naïla Waltz**) and
      the second act of **La source** (into which the divertis-
      sement was later incorporated). This is the best
      material on the ballet.

109. Guest, Ivor. **The Ballet of the Second Empire (1858–
      1870).** London: Black, 1953, pp. 93–99. Cita-
      tion also used following items 120 and 151.
      GV 1649.G8

      Very good historical material on **La source.**

110. Hering, Doris. "New York City Ballet: Some High-
      lights." **Dance Magazine** 43 (April 1969): 85.

      Short description of the performance of Balanchine's
      Pas de deux: La source.

*   Poueigh, Jean. **Musiciens français d'aujourd'hui,**
      p. 150. Cited above as item 47.

      Sample of manuscript from **La source.**

111. **The Simon and Schuster Book of the Ballet: A Complete
      Reference Guide, 1581 to the Present.** New York:
      Simon and Schuster, 1980, pp. 130–32. Citation
      also used following items 176 and 238.
      GV 1787.B275313   ISBN 067141223X

      History and plot; translation of **Il balletto:
      Repertorio del teatro di danza dal 1581.**

112. Vaillat, Léandre. **Ballets de l'Opéra de Paris.**
Paris: Compagnie française des arts graphiques,
1943. Citation also used following item 238.

This book on the ballets performed at the Paris
Opéra contains some material on **La source.**

113. Wolff, Stéphane. **L'Opéra au Palais Garnier, 1875–
1962: Les oeuvres, les interprètes.** Paris:
L'Entr'acte, 1962, p. 326. Citation also used
following items 186, 239, 259, and 261.
ML 1727.8.P2 W8

Valuable basic data on **La source** as performed at
the Palais Garnier.

2. Scenarios

114. Nuitter, Charles [Charles Truinet], and Arthur Saint-
Léon. **La sorgente: Ballo fantastico in 3 atti e
5 quadri.** Milan: Ricordi, [1875?].

115. ———— . **La sorgente: Ballo fantastico in tre atti
e quattro quadri.** Bologna: Socièta Tip. dei com-
positori, 1877.

116. ———— . **La sorgente: Ballo fantastico in 3 atti e
5 quadri.** Milan: Ricordi, [1887?].

117. ———— . **La source: Ballet en trois actes et quatre
tableaux.** Paris: Librairie dramatique, 1866.

3. Choreography

118. **Choreography by George Balanchine: A Catalogue of
Works.** New York: Viking, 1984, pp. 244–45, 253,
265–67. Citation was also used following items
120, 195, 242, 262, and 346.
GV 1785.B32 C49 1984   ISBN 0670220086

On Balanchine's choreography for **La source** (page
253), and the use of parts of **La source** in **Pas de
Deux and Divertissement** (pages 244–45) and in **Coppélia**
(pages 265–670). Another edition was published in 1983
by Eakins Press Foundation, New York.

4. Dancers and dance companies
in relation to **La source**

119. Huckenpahler, Victoria. **Ballerina: A Biography of
Violette Verdy.** New York: Audience Arts, 1978.

GV 1785.V47 H83   ISBN 0824765184

Biography of the ballerina, with material on her
performance in **La source.**

120. Reynolds, Nancy. **Repertory in Review: 40 Years of
     the New York City Ballet.** New York: Dial Press,
     1977, pp. 230, 256-57. Citation also used fol-
     lowing items 218, 245, and 263.
     GV 1786.N4 R48   ISBN 0803773684

On the company's performance of **La source** (pages
256-57) and its use of part of **La source** in **Pas de
Deux and Divertissement** (page 230).

VALSE, OU, PAS DES FLEURS

(See also Flourescences, Pas de Deux and
Divertissement, and Le jardin animé)

*   **Choreography by George Balanchine,** pp. 196-97, 244-45,
     253. cited above as item 118.

On Balanchine's choreography for **Pas de fleurs**
(**Naïla Waltz**) (pages 196-97) and the use of the waltz
in **Pas de Deux and Divertissement** (pages 244-45) and
La source (page 253).

*   Dunn, Thomas D. "Delibes and La Source," pp. 9, 11.
     Cited above as item 108.

On the confusion between the 1867 **Pas des fleurs**
divertissement (also called **Naïla Waltz**) and a part
of the second act of **La source** (also called **Naïla**).

*   Guest, Ivor. **The Ballet of the Second Empire (1858-
     1870),** p. 102. Cited above as item 109.
     GV 1649.G8

On the history of **Pas des fleurs.**

COPPÉLIA

1. History, plots, other general works

(The history and plot materials below, which vary in
content, were selected from a wide body of literature)

121. Abrahams, Doris Caroline [Caryl Brahms, pseud.].
     Coppelia: The Story of the Ballet Told for the Young.
     London: Haverstock, [19--].

Illustrated juvenile story of the ballet.

122.   ———— . Coppélia: The Story of the Ballet Told For
        the Young. London: Sylvan Press, 1946.

        Another edition of item 121.

123.   Almanach des Königl. Hof. und National-Theaters und
        des Königl. Residenz-Theaters zu München für das
        Jahr 1892. Munich: Bruckmann'sche Buchdruckerei,
        1893.

        Yearbook containing some material on the perfor-
        mance of Coppélia in Munich.

124.   Balanchine, George. Balanchine's Complete Stories of
        the Great Ballets. Edited by Francis Mason.
        Garden City, N.Y.: Doubleday, 1954, pp. 95-109.
        Citation also used following item 226.
        MT 95.B3

        History and plot.

125.   ———— . Balanchine's New Complete Stories of the
        Great Ballets. Edited by Francis Mason. Garden City,
        N.Y.: Doubleday, 1968, pp. 96-103. Citation also
        used following item 226.
        MT 95.B3   1968

        History and plot.

*   Balanchine, George, and Francis Mason. Balanchine's
        Complete Stories of the Great Ballets, pp. 100,
        130-43. Cited above as item 102.

        History and plot of Coppélia (pages 130-143) and
        use of the pas de deux from Coppélia in the ballet
        Celebration (page 100).

126.   ———— . 101 Stories of Great Ballets. Garden City,
        N.Y.: Dolphin Books, 1975, pp. 47, 75-92. Cita-
        tion also following item 263.
        MT 95.B3   1975   ISBN 0385033982

        History and plot of Coppélia (pages 75-92) and use
        of the pas de deux from Coppélia in the ballet
        Celebration (page 47).

127.   Beaumont, Cyril W. Ballet Design, Past & Present.
        London: Studio, 1946.
        GV 1787.B33

        This well-illustrated treatise on ballet sets and
        costumes includes material on Coppélia.

*   _____ . **Complete Book of Ballets,** pp. 593–600.
            Cited above as item 104.

            History and plot.

*   _____ . **Complete Book of Ballets,** pp. 483–89. Cited
            above as item·105.

            History and plot.

128.   _____ . **Dancers Under My Lens: Essays in Ballet
            Criticism.** London: C.W. Beaumont, 1949, pp. 90–95.
            GV 1787.B375

            History and criticism of **Coppélia.**

129.   Bethléem, L. [and others]. **Les opéras, les opéras-
            comique, et les opérettes.** Paris: Editions de la
            revue de lectures, 1926, pp. 142–43. Citation also
            used following items 227, 278, 300, 304, and 347.
            ML 1700.B38

            History and plot.

130.   Borská, Ilona. **Coppélia.** Translated by Anna
            Albertová. Munich: Südwest Verlag, 1971.

            Illustrated juvenile book on **Coppélia.**

131.   _____ . **Coppélia.** English version based on trans-
            lation by Yvonne Sebest'áková. New York: Watts,
            1971.
            ML 3930.D4   B7

            English version of item 130.

132.   _____ . **Coppélia; D'après Léo Delibes.** 2d ed.
            Paris: Gründ, 1978.

            French version of item 130.

*   Brilliant, Maurice. "Du romanticisme à Jacques
            Rouché," pp. 75–77. Cited above as item 106.

            On the history of **Coppélia.**

133.   Brinson, Peter. **Background to European Ballet: A
            Notebook from Its Archives.** Leyden: Sijthoff,
            1966, pp. 67–69.
            GV 1787.B66

            On the original production of **Coppélia.**

134. Brinson, Peter, and Clement Crisp. **The International
      Book of Ballet.** New York: Stein and Day, 1971,
      pp. 35-38.
      MT 95.B79 1971   ISBN 0812813316

      History and plot. A 1970 London edition was pub-
      lished under the title **Ballet for All.**

135. Buckle, Richard. **Modern Ballet Design: A Picture-
      book with Notes.** New York: Macmillan, 1955,
      pp. 102, 104, 120-21. Citation also used following
      item 228.

      On ballet scenery and costume for **Coppélia,** with
      good illustrations. Another edition was published in
      1955 by Black, London.

136. Bury, H. Blaze de. "Coppélia." **Revue des deux mondes**
      (June 15, 1870).

      On the original production of **Coppélia.**

137. Chappell, Warren. **Coppélia, the Girl with Enamel Eyes.**
      Knopf, 1965.
      ML 3930.D4 C5

      Juvenile book, with illustrations, containing the
      plot and some of the musical themes.

138. Clarke, Mary, and Clement Crisp. **The Ballet Goer's
      Guide.** New York: Knopf, 1981, pp. 98-101.
      GV 1787.C563 1981   ISBN 039451307X

      History and plot.

139. **Coppélia.** L'Avant-scène ballet/danse, vol. 4
      Paris: L'Avant-scène, 1981. 119 p.
      GV 1580.A9 vol. 4

      Best book on **Coppélia,** containing articles (in
      French) on: dolls, etc. used in romantic era produc-
      tions; extended story of the ballet; musical commen-
      tary; contemporary criticism; background on the
      ballet; history of performance; and chronology of
      performance. It also has an excellent bibliography,
      and discography, and many illustrations, including a
      facsimile of a program.

140. Crosland, Margaret. **Ballet Carnival: A Companion to
      Ballet.** London: Arco, 1957, pp. 141-47. Cita-
      tion also used following item 230.

164   Bibliography

History and plot. Another edition was published in
1955.

141. Crowle, Pigeon. **Tales from the Ballet.** London:
      Faber & Faber, 1953, pp. 65–80.
      MT 95.C8 1953

      History and plot. Another edition was published in
      1953 by Pitman, New York.

142. Davidson, Gladys. **Stories of the Ballets.** London:
      W. Laurie, 1958, pp. 318–26, 468–69. Citation also
      used following item 231.

      Pages 318–326 give the plot of **Coppélia,** and pages
      468–469 give some historical data and a list of pro-
      ductions. Another edition was published by Laurie in
      1949.

143. Denby, Edwin. **Looking at the Dance.** New York:
      Horizon Press, 1968.
      GV 1787.D43 1968

      Contains some material on the history and criticism
      of **Coppélia,** particularly pages 84–87 which have a
      good analysis of the purpose and psychology of the
      ballet, emphasizing the theme of marriage.

144. Detaille, Georges, and Gérard Mulys. **Les ballets de
      Monte-Carlo, 1911–1944.** Paris: Editions Arc-en-
      ciel, 1954, pp. 196–99, 238–39.

      History and plot of **Coppélia** as performed in Monte
      Carlo.

*   Drew, David, ed. **The Decca Book of Ballet,** pp. 120–26.
      Cited above as item 107.

      History, plot, and musical themes.

145. Ewen, David. **The Complete Book of Classical Music.**
      Englewood Cliffs, N.J.: Prentice-Hall, 1965,
      pp. 653–54. Citation also used following items 232
      and 314.

      History and plot. A short general essay on Delibes
      is on pages 652–653.

146. _____ . **The Encyclopedia of Musical Masterpieces:
      Music for the Millions.** New York: Grosset &
      Dunlap, 1949, pp. 179–80. Citation also used

following item 314.

Well-written reference article. Other editions
were published under the title **Music for the Millions.**

147. ———. **Ewen's Musical Masterworks: The Encyclopedia of Musical Masterpieces.** 2d ed. New York:
Arco, 1954, pp. 197-98. Citation also used
following item 314.
MT 90.E9 M8 1954

Well-written reference article.

148. Gadan-Pamard, Francis, and Robert Maillard, eds.
Dictionary of Modern Ballet. Translated from the
French by John Montague and Peggie Cochrane. New
York: Tudor Publishing Co., 1959, pp. 99-101. Ci-
tation also used following item 233.
GV 1787.D513

Very good reference article (translation of item
149). Another English edition was published in 1959
by Methuen, London.

149. ———. **Dictionnaire du ballet moderne.** Paris:
F. Hazan, 1957. Citation also used following item
233.
GV 1787.D5

Has a very good reference article on **Coppélia.**
Item 148 is the English translation.

150. Goode, Gerald, ed. **The Book of Ballets, Classic and
Modern.** New York: Crown, 1939, pp. 73-77.
MT 95.G7

History and plot, with three musical themes.

151. Gruen, John. **The World's Great Ballets: La fille
mal gardée to Davidsbündlertänze.** New York:
Abrams, 1981, pp. 37-40.
GV 1790.A1 G78   ISBN 0810907259

History and plot.

* Guest, Ivor. **The Ballet of the Second Empire (1858-
1870),** pp. 107-31. Cited above as item 109.

Very good historical material on **Coppélia.** This
and the item following 158 are perhaps the best general English-language essays on the ballet.

152. _____ . "The Birth of 'Coppélia'." **Dance Magazine**
      32 (February 1958): 52–53, 67.

      Fine essay on **Coppélia** and Guiseppina Bozzacchi,
      the first ballerina to perform the lead role.

153. _____ . **Two Coppélias: A Centenary Study to Mark
      the One Hundredth Anniversary of the Ballet Coppélia
      and Accompany a Centenary Production of Two Cop-
      pélias by the Royal Ballet's Ballet for All.**
      London: Friends of Covent Garden, 1970.

      48 page book on the history of **Coppélia** published
      on the occasion of the ballet's one hundredth anni-
      versary. The two **Coppélias** are a French production
      and a Russian production.

154. Hall, George. **The Story of the Ballet: Coppélia.**
      London: Ballet Books, [196–?].

      24 page story of **Coppélia**.

155. Jackson, Sheila. **Ballet in England: A Book of Litho-
      graphs.** London: Transatlantic Arts, 1945.

      Mostly illustrations of individual ballets, with
      some text; includes material on **Coppélia**.

156. Kerensky, Oleg. **Ballet Scene.** London: H. Hamilton,
      1970, pp. 23–24.
      GV 1787.K37 1970   ISBN 0241018773

      Good general information on **Coppélia**. This is
      identical to item 158.

157. _____ . **The Guinness Guide to Ballet.** Enfield,
      Middlesex: Guinness Superlatives Ltd., 1981, pp.
      164–65.
      GV 1787.K36   ISBN 0851122264

      History, analysis, and plot.

158. _____ . **The World of Ballet.** New York: Coward–
      McCann, 1970, pp. 25–26.
      GV 1787.K37 1970b

      Good general information on **Coppélia**. This is
      identical to item 156.

*   Kirstein, Lincoln. "Léo Delibes and the Inscape of
         Coppélia" pp. 28-29, 38. Cited above as item 32.

         Excellent essay, very favorable to Delibes, on
         Coppélia and its composer. This and the item
         following 151 are perhaps the best general English-
         language essays on the ballet.

159.   ——— . **Movement & Metaphor: Four Centuries of
         Ballet.** New York: Praeger, 1970, pp. 170-73.
         GV 1787. K513

         Well-written section on the history of **Coppélia**.

160. Krokover, Rosalyn. **The New Borzoi Book of Ballets.**
         New York: Knopf, 1956, pp. 73-79.
         MT 95.K76

         History and plot.

161. Lawrence, Robert. **The Victor Book of Ballets and
         Ballet Music.** New York: Simon and Schuster, 1950,
         pp. 119-26. Citation also used following item 236.
         MT 95.L48

         History and plot, with several musical themes.

162. Levinson, Andreĭ IAkovlevich. **La danse au théâtre:
         Esthétique et actualité mêlées.** Paris: Librairie
         Bloud & Gay, 1924, pp. 113-15. Citation also used
         following item 236.
         GV 1781.L4

         Commentary on **Coppélia**.

163. Mannoni, Gérard. **Grands ballets de l'Opéra de Paris.**
         Paris: Sylvie Messinger et Théâtre national de
         l'Opéra de Paris, 1982, pp. 80-101. Citation also
         used following item 236.

         Well-illustrated excellent comprehensive essay on
         Coppélia; one of the best sources taking into account
         the combination of quality, quantity, and scope.

164. Martin, John Joseph. "Reports from Russia." **Dance
         Magazine** 30 (September 1956): 14-21, 58-64.

         Has material on the Russian production of **Coppélia**.

165. Moore, Lillian. "The First 'Swanhilda'." **Dancing
         Times,** no. 348 (September 1939): 616-17.

Good article on the brief life of Guiseppina
Bozzacchi, the 16 year old who was the first person
to dance the role of Swanilda in **Coppélia,** and who
died only three months after the debut.

166. "100 Years of Coppélia." **Dance and Dancers** 21 (June
      1970): 30–31.

      Brief but informative history of the performance of
      Coppélia, with several very good photographs.

167. Posner, Sandy. **Coppélia: The Story of the Ballet.**
      London: Newman Wolsey, 1946.

      95 page illustrated story of the ballet. At least
      3 other editions were published.

168. "Principales versions chorégraphiques de Coppélia sur
      la musique de Léo Delibes." **Pour la danse: Chaus-
      sons & petits rats,** no. 47 (December 1978–January
      1979): 8–9.

      Chart listing the various versions of **Coppélia** from
      1870 to 1977.

169. Rebling, Eberhard. **Ballet von A bis Z.** Berlin:
      Henschel, 1966, pp. 42–47.
      MT 95.R33

      History and plot.

170. Regner, Otto Friedrich, ed. **Reclams Balletführer.**
      Stuttgart: Reclam-Verlag, 1956, pp. 64–73. Cita-
      tation also used following item 237.

      History and plot. At least five editions were
      published.

171. Reyer, Ernest. "Coppélia." **Journal des débats**
      (December 26, 1882).

      Contemporary commentary on **Coppélia.**

172. Reynolds, Nancy, and Susan Reimer-Torn. **In Per-
      formance: A Companion to the Classics of the
      Dance.** New York: Harmony Books, 1980, pp. 46–52.
      GV 1781.R44 1980   ISBN 0517539926

      History and plot.

173. Robert, Grace. **The Borzoi Book of Ballets.** New York:
      Knopf, 1946, pp. 84–94.

GV 1787.R6

History and plot.

174. Roseveare, Ursula. **Selected Stories from the Ballet.**
London: Pitman, 1954, pp. 41-52. Citation also
used following item 238.
MT 95.R76

History and plot for a juvenile audience.

175. Sato, Satoru. **Leo Delibes' Coppelia: Based on Leo
Delibes' Ballet After the Story by E.T.A. Hoffmann.**
Tokyo: Gakken, 1970.
ML 3930.D4   S3

Illustrated story of the ballet for juveniles, as
adapted by Sato. Another edition was published in
1973 by F. Warne, London.

176. Severn, Merlyn, and Arnold L. Haskell. **Ballet in
Action.** London: J. Lane, 1938, pp. 15, 117.

Material on performance of **Coppélia**, with photos by
Severn and some text by Haskell.

*   **The Simon and Schuster Book of the Ballet**, pp. 133-
35. Cited above as item 111.

History and plot.

177. **100 [Sto] baletnykh libretto.** Moscow: Muzyka, 1966,
pp. 95-99. Citation also used following item 238.
ML 48.S72

History and plot.

178. Tardy-Marcus, Julia. "Die erste Coppélia:
Erinnerungen an ein tanzendes Kind und seine
Epoch." **Neue Zürcher Zeitung** 21/22 (June 1975):
59.

About Giuseppina Bozzacchi, the first dancer to
perform the lead role in **Coppélia**, and also about the
premiere of the ballet.

179. Terry, Walter. **Ballet: A New Guide to the Liveliest
Art.** New York: Dell, 1959, pp. 97-101. Citation
also used following item 238.
GV 1787.T32

Well-written history and plot.

180. _____ . **Ballet Guide: Background, Listings,
      Credits, and Descriptions of More Than Five Hundred
      of the World's Major Ballets.** New York: Dodd,
      Mead, 1976, pp. 94–98. Citation also used fol-
      lowing item 238.
      GV 1790.A1 T47   ISBN 0396070248

      History and plot.

181. _____ . "World of Dance: Comedy Classic." **Saturday
      Review** 53 (June 6, 1970): 51.

      Very good article on the history of **Coppélia**, plus
      a description of a 100th birthday performance by the
      Boston Ballet.

182. Untermeyer, Louis. **Tales from the Ballet.** New York:
      Golden Press, 1968, pp. 54–60.
      ML 3930.A2 U5

      Illustrated juvenile story of **Coppélia**.

183. Vaillat, Léandre. **Ballets de l'Opéra de Paris:
      Ballets dans les opéras, nouveaux ballets.**
      Paris: Compagnie française des arts graphiques,
      1947.

      Has some material on **Coppélia** as performed at the
      Paris Opéra. This is a different publication from his
      1943 book of the same title (item 112).

184. Verwer, Hans. **Guide to the Ballet.** Translated from
      the Dutch by Henry Mins. New York: Barnes and
      Noble, 1963, pp. 45–50. Citation also used
      following item 238.
      GV 1787.V383

      History and plot.

185. Viveash, Cherry. **Tales from the Ballet.** London:
      G. Ronald, 1958, pp. 33–41. Citation also used
      following item 238.

      History and plot.

186. Winkler, H.J. **Oper und Ballett.** Munich: Südwest
      Verlag, 1964, pp. 371–73. Citation also used fol-
      lowing item 239.

      History and plot.

*   Wolff, Stéphane. **L'Opéra au Palais Garnier, 1875–
      1962,** pp. 258–59. Cited above as item 113.

      Valuable basic data on **Coppélia** as performed at
      the Palais Garnier.

2. Scenarios

187. Nuitter, Charles [Charles Truinet], and Arthur Saint-
      Léon. **Coppélia: Balett i två akter.** Stockholm:
      Stellan Ståls Boktryckeri, 1899.

188. ———— . **Coppelia: Grand Ballet in Three Acts.**
      New York: C.S. Koppel, 1886.

189. ———— . **Coppelia: Grand Ballet in Three Acts.**
      New York: F. Rullman, 1908.

190. ———— . **Coppelia, o, La fanciulla dagli occhi di
      smalto: Azione coregrafica in due atti.** Milan:
      E. Sonzogno, 1894.

191. ———— . **Coppelia, o, La fanciulla dagli occhi di
      smalto: Azione coregrafica in due atti e tre
      quadri.** Milan: E. Sonzogno, 1885.

192. ———— . **Coppélia, oder, Das Mädchen mit den Emaille-
      Augen: Ballett in 2 Abtheilungen.** Berlin:
      A. Fürstner, [ca. 1885].

193. ———— . **Coppélia, ou, La fille aux yeux d'émail:
      Ballet en deux actes et trois tableaux.** Paris:
      E. Dentu, 1870.

194. ———— . **Scenario of Coppelia: A ballet pantomime.**
      [New York?, 19—-].

3. Music

195. Fiske, Roger. **Ballet Music.** London: G. Harrap,
      1958, pp. 22–31. Citation also used following
      item 241.
      MT 95.F5

      Excellent commentary on the music of **Coppélia,** with
      21 musical themes given. It is perhaps the best
      treatment of the ballet's music.

4. Choreography

*   **Choreography by George Balanchine,** pp. 206, 265–67.
       Cited above as item 118.

       On Balanchine's choreography for **One, Yuletide
       Square,** a television abridgement of **Coppélia** (page
       206), and a full **Coppélia** (pages 265–67).

196.   **Coppelia Collection.** New York: Dance Notation
       Bureau, 1970.

       Dance notation for four dances from Coppélia.

197.   Ivanov, Lev Ivanovich. **The Dance of Work, Betrothal
       Dance, from Coppelia, Act III.** [New York?,
       1959?].

       Dance notation for two dances from **Coppélia.** The
       choreography is by Ivanov and Enrico Cecchetti, and
       the notation by Richard Ellis and Christine DuBoulay.

198.   ——— . **The Dances of Swanilda and Her Friends, From
       Coppelia, Act. I.** [New York?, 1959?].

       Dance notation for Act I of **Coppélia,** with the
       choreography by Ivanov and the notation by Richard
       Ellis and Christine DuBoulay.

199.   Martínez, Enrique. **Coppelia: Ballet in Three Acts.**
       New York: Dance Notation Bureau, 1977.

       Dance notation for **Coppélia,** with choreography by
       Martínez.

200.   McDonagh, Don. **George Balanchine.** Boston: Twayne,
       1983.

       Biography of the choreographer, with some material
       on **Coppélia.**

201.   Pilkington, Linda, ed. **Dances from the Classics.**
       London: College of Choreology, 1967.

       Includes dance notation for part of **Coppélia.**

202.   Saint–Léon, Arthur. **Coppelia.** [New York: Dance
       Notation Bureau], 1972.

       Dance notation for **Coppélia,** with choreography by
       André Eglevsky after Saint–Léon.

203. ———— . **The Scotch Dance from Coppelia, Act II, the**
      Dance of the Hours from Coppelia, Act III.
      [New York?, 1959?].

      Dance notation for two dances from **Coppélia**, with
      choreography by Saint-Léon and dance notation by
      Richard Ellis and Christine DuBoulay.

204. Vaughan, David. **Frederick Ashton and His Ballets.**
      London: Black, 1977. Citation also used following
      item 242.
      GV 1785.A8 V38 1977b   ISBN 071361689X

      Has some material on the choreography for **Coppélia**
      as done by Ashton. Another edition was published in
      1977 by Knopf, New York.

                    5. Dancers and dance companies
                        in relation to **Coppélia**

         (The following is a selective sample. Many works
              on dancers and dance companies contain
                        relevant material)

205. Benois, Alexander. **Reminiscences of the Russian**
      Ballet. London: Putnam, 1941, pp. 64-69. Cita-
      tion also used following item 242.
      GV 1787.B49

      On **Coppélia** as performed in Russia. The memoirs
      cover the late 19th and early 20th centuries.

206. Bland, Alexander. **The Nureyev Image.** London: Studio
      Vista, 1976.
      GV 1785.N8 B57   ISBN 028970362X

      Photo-biography of the dancer, including material
      on his performance in **Coppélia**. Another edition was
      published by Quadrangle, New York.

207. Clarke, Mary. **The Sadler's Wells Ballet: A History**
      and an Appreciation. London: Black, 1955. Cita-
      tion also used following item 243.
      GV 1786.S3 C6

      History of the company, with some material on
      Coppélia. Another edition was published in 1955 by
      Macmillan, New York.

208. Crowle, Pigeon. **Moira Shearer: Portrait of a Dancer.**
      London: Faber & Faber, 1951.

      Includes text and photos on the ballerina's perform-
      ance in **Coppélia**. Another edition was published by
      Faber & Faber in 1949, and by Pitman, New York, in 1951.

209. Fisher, Hugh. **The Sadler's Wells Theatre Ballet.**
      London: Black, 1956, pp. 48–49, 66–67.
      GV 1786.S3   F49

      On the company's performance of **Coppélia** during
      the 1946–1956 period. Another edition was published
      in 1956 by Pitman, New York.

210. Franks, Arthur Henry. **Svetlana Beriosova: A**
      Biography. London: Burke, 1958. Citation also
      used following item 243.
      GV 1785.B44   F7

      Biography of the ballerina, with material on her
      performance in **Coppélia.**

211. Gillard, David. **Beryl Grey: A Biography.** London:
      W.H. Allen, 1977. Citation also used following
      item 243.
      GV 1785.G72   G54   ISBN 0491022212

      Biography of the ballerina, with material on her
      performance in **Coppélia.**

212. Goldner, Nancy, and Lincoln Kirstein. **Coppelia: New**
      York City Ballet. New York: Eakins Press
      Foundation, 1974.
      GV 1790.C66   G64   ISBN 0871300427

      Small work, with photos, on **Coppélia** as performed
      by the New York City Ballet.

213. Gruen, John. **Erik Bruhn, Danseur Noble.** New York:
      Viking Press, 1979.
      GV 1785.B78   G78   ISBN 0670297712

      Biography of the dancer, with material on his
      performance in **Coppélia.**

214. Guest, Ivor. **Adeline Genée: A Lifetime of Ballet**
      under Six Reigns. London: Black, 1958.
      GV 1785.G383   G8

      Biography of the ballerina, with some material on
      Coppélia.

215. _____ . **The Divine Virginia: A Biography of Virginia**
      Zucchi. New York: Dekker, 1977.
      GV 1785.Z82   G83   ISBN 0824764927

      Biography of the ballerina, with some material on

Coppélia.

216. Makarova, Natalia. **A Dance Autobiography.** New York:
     Knopf, 1979.
     GV 1785.M26 A35 1979   ISBN 0394501411

     Autobiography of the ballerina, with some material
     on her performance in **Coppélia.**

217. Money, Keith. **The Art of the Royal Ballet as seen by
     Keith Money.** Cleveland: World Publishing Co.,
     1967, pp. 210–27. Citation also used following item
     245.

     Mostly pictorial treatment of the Royal Ballet's
     performance of **Coppélia.** Another edition was
     published by G. Harrap, London.

218. ———— . **Fonteyn, the Making of a Legend.** London:
     Collins, 1973, pp. 103–05. Citation also used
     following item 245.
     GV 1785.F63 M65

     On the ballerina's performance in **Coppélia.**

* Reynolds, Nancy. **Repertory in Review,** pp. 314–19.
     Cited above as item 120.

     On the New York City Ballet's performance of
     Coppélia.

219. Terry, Walter. **Alicia and Her Ballet Nacional de Cuba:
     An Illustrated Biography of Alicia Alonso.** Garden
     City, N.Y.: Anchor Books, 1981.
     GV 1785.A63 T47   ISBN 0385149565

     Biography of the ballerina, with a fair amount of
     material on her performance in **Coppélia.**

6. Movies and videotapes

220. Braun, Susan, and Jessie Kitching, comps. **Dance and
     Mime Film and Videotape Catalog.** New York: Dance
     Films Association, 1980, pp. 7, 11, 19, 31, 40, 68.
     Citation also used following item 247.
     GV 1594.D364 1980

     Annotations on movie and videotape versions of
     Coppélia.

221. Mueller, John. **Dance Film Directory: An Annotated**

and Evaluative Guide to Films on Ballet and Modern
Dance. Princeton, N.J.: Princeton Book Co., 1979,
pp. 31, 36.
GV 1595.M89   ISBN 9016622088

Evaluations of movie versions of Coppélia.

222. Ten Years of Films on Ballet and Classical Dance,
     1956-1965: Catalogue. Paris: Unesco, 1968.
     GV 1790.Al T4

This annotated catalog of dance movies, arranged by
country, includes entries for Coppélia.

7.   Derivatives, adaptations, etc.

(See also Celebration)

223. Griffiths, Philip, and Eric Shaw. My Daughter
     Coppelia: A Musical Play (Adapted from Delibes'
     Ballet Coppelia). London: Oxford University
     Press, 1971.
     ML 50.G8553 M9 1971   ISBN 0193382288

Libretto of musical based on Coppélia.

SYLVIA

1.   History, plots, other general works

(The history and plot materials below, which
vary in content, were selected from a
wide body of literature)

224. Adler, Henry. "Revival of Sylvia Stresses Interest of
     Sadler's Wells in Full-Length Ballets." Musical
     America 73 (November 1, 1953): 7.

Short essay on Sylvia and its revival. A review
of the Sadler's Wells production follows.

225. _____ . "'Sylvia' Completes a Long Cycle of Ballet
     History." Dance News 23 (October 1953): 5.

Well-written and informative concise history of
Sylvia, on the occasion of the first full-length
Sylvia in England (1952).

226. Almanach des Königl. Hof. und National-Theaters und
     des Königl. Residenz-Theaters zu München für das
     Jahr 1883, 1887. Munich: Wolf, Kgl. Hof. und
     Universitäts Buchdruckerei, 1884, 1888.

Two yearbooks with some material on the performance
of Sylvia in Munich.

*   Balanchine, George. Balanchine's Complete Stories of

the Great Ballets, pp. 390–93. Cited above as item 124.

History and plot.

*   ———— . Balanchine's New Complete Stories of the Great Ballets, pp. 424–27. Cited above as item 125.

History and plot.

*   Balanchine, George, and Francis Mason. Balanchine's Complete Stories of the Great Ballets, pp. 616–20. Cited above as item 102.

History and plot.

227. Beaumont, Cyril W. Ballets of Today: Being a Second Supplement to the Complete Book of Ballets. London: Putnam, 1954, pp. 29–36. MT 95.B39

History and plot.

*   ———— . Complete Book of Ballets, pp. 600–08. Cited above as item 104.

History and plot; this, the following item, and items 232 and 239 are perhaps the best general English-language material on the ballet.

*   ———— . Complete Book of Ballets, pp. 489–96. Cited above as item 105.

History and plot; see the annotation for the previous item.

*   Bethléem, L. [and others]. Les opéras, les opéras-comiques, et les opérettes, p. 145. Cited above as item 129.

History and plot.

*   Brillant, Maurice. "Du romanticisme à Jacques Rouché," pp. 80–81. Cited above as item 106.

On the history of Sylvia.

228. Buckle, Richard. The Adventures of a Ballet Critic. London: Cresset Press, 1953, pp. 113–14. GV 1787.B8

Relates the story of the author's unused proposals
for severely modifying a planned production of **Sylvia**
(1952).

*   ____ . **Modern Ballet Design**, pp. 80-90. Cited
    above as item 135.

On ballet scenery and costumes for **Sylvia**, with
good illustrations.

229. Bury, H. Blaze de. "Sylvia." **Revue de deux mondes**
     (July 1, 1876).

On the original production of **Sylvia**.

230. Christout, Marie Françoise, and John Percival. "Paris
     Opéra Ballet at the Théâtre de L'Opéra." **Dance**
     and Dancers 30 (December 1979): 31-33.

Two good articles on the performance of **Sylvia** in
Paris, with a fair amount of informative historical
material.

*   Crosland, Margaret. **Ballet Carnival**, pp. 355-58.
    Cited above as item 140.

History and plot.

231. Crowle, Pigeon. **Come to the Ballet.** London: Faber &
     Faber, 1957, pp. 117-27.
     MT 95.C792

History and plot. Another edition was published in
1957 by Pitman, New York.

*   Davidson, Gladys. **Stories of the Ballets,** pp. 327-
     35, 484. Cited above as item 142.

Pages 327-335 give the plot of **Sylvia**, and page 484
gives some historical data and a list of productions.

*   Drew, David, ed. **The Decca Book of Ballet**, pp. 130-
     35. Cited above as item 107.

History, plot, and musical themes.

232. Evans, Edwin. "Who is Sylvia?" **Dancing Times,** no.
     407 (August 1944): 493-94.

Excellent article on **Sylvia**, very favorable to the
music. Included are some interesting quotes derived
from contemporary criticism of the ballet. Two of the

more provocative statements were the comments that
Sylvia was Wagnerian and that the music might be too
good to use in ballet. Also dealt with are Tchaikovsky's very high opinion of **Sylvia** and Evan's claim
that Tchaikovsky did not borrow his ideas for ballet
from Delibes. This and item 239 are perhaps the best
general English-language essays on the ballet, along
with Beaumont's **Complete Book of Ballets.**

*   Ewen, David. **The Complete Book of Classical Music,**
      pp. 654-55. Cited above as item 145.

      History and plot. A short general essay on Delibes
      is on pages 652-653.

233. Fuld, James J. **The Book of World-Famous Music:**
      Classical, Popular and Folk. New York: Crown,
      1966, pp. 355-56. Citation also used following
      item 316.
      ML 113.F8

      On the pizzicati from **Sylvia.**

*   Gadan-Pamard, Francis, and Robert Maillard, eds.
      Dictionary of Modern Ballet, p. 330. Cited above
      as item 148.

      Brief but good reference article (translation of
      the following item). The music is described as "tune-
      ful, colourful and admirably orchestrated." Also, the
      music is said to have had "considerable influence on
      Tchaikovsky."

*   ———— . **Dictionnaire du ballet moderne.** Cited above
      as item 149.

      Has a brief but good reference article on **Sylvia.**
      The previous item is the English translation.

234. Jouvin, B. "Sylvia." **Le figaro** (June 15, 1876).

      On the original production of **Sylvia.**

235. Jullien, Adolphe. **Musiciens d'aujourd'hui.** 2d series.
      Paris: Librairie de l'art, 1894, pp. 261-66.
      Citation also used following items 303, 320, 347,
      and 350.
      ML 390.J94

      Interesting history of and commentary on **Sylvia.**

236. Koegler, Horst. "The Hungarian State Ballet at the
     Budapest Opera House." **Dance and Dancers** 24
     (August 1973): 52-54, 56.

     On the performance of **Sylvia** in Budapest. The
     principal value of the article is the author's very
     good understanding of the ballet.

*   Lawrence, Robert. **The Victor Book of Ballets and
     Ballet Music**, pp. 454-57. Cited above as item 161.

     History and plot with several musical themes.

*   Levinson, Andreĭ IАkovlevich. **La danse aux théâtre**,
     pp. 82-87, 269-71. Cited above as item 162.

     Commentary on **Sylvia**.

*   Mannoni, Gérard. **Grands ballets de l'Opéra de Paris**,
     pp. 102-21. Cited above as item 163.

     Well-illustrated excellent comprehensive essay on
     Sylvia; possibly the best overall source on the bal-
     let, taking into account the combination of quality,
     quantity, and scope.

237. Moreno, H. "Sylvia, ou, La nymphe de Diane." **Le
     ménestrel** 42 (June 18, 1876): 226-28.

     On the original production of **Sylvia**.

*   Regner, Otto Friedrich, ed. **Reclams Balletführer**,
     pp. 350-55. Cited above as item 170.

     History and plot.

238. Reyer, Ernest. "Sylvia." **Journal des débats**
     (June 26, 1892).

     Contemporary commentary on **Sylvia**.

*   Rohozinski, Ladislas, ed. **Cinquante ans de musique
     française, de 1874 à 1925**, vol. 1, pp. 39-41.
     Cited above as item 52.

     Good material on the history of **Sylvia**, including
     one illustration of a stage setting.

*   Roseveare, Ursula. **Selected Stories from the Ballet**,
     pp. 104-10. Cited above as item 174.

     History and plot for a juvenile audience.

86.N4   H5

...n the New York City Ballet in performance, with
...text by Terry and many photos by Himmel. Some
...rial on **Sylvia pas de deux** is included.

...even, Peter. **The Birth of Ballets-Russes.**
Translated by L. Zarine. New York: Dover, 1973,
pp. 40-42.

On Sergei Daighilev and the scandal over the production of **Sylvia** in Russia in 1901. The same
incident is reported in the item immediately preceding
item 243. Another edition was published in 1936 by
Allen & Unwin, London.

Money, Keith. **The Art of the Royal Ballet as Seen by
Keith Money**, pp. 38-57. Cited above as item 217.

Mostly pictorial treatment of the Royal Ballet's
performance of **Sylvia.**

_____ . **Fonteyn, the Making of a Legend**, pp. 142-43.
Cited above as item 218.

On the ballerina's performance in **Sylvia.**

*   Reynolds, Nancy. **Repertory in Review**, pp. 116-17.
Cited above as item 120.

On the New York City Ballet's performance of **Sylvia
pas de deux.**

246. Roné, Elvira. **Olga Preobrazhenskaya: A Portrait.**
Translated, adapted, and introduced by Fernau Hall.
New York: Dekker, 1978, pp. 48-51.
GV 1785.P7 H34

ISBN 0824766636

On the ballerina's performance in **Sylvia.**

247. **Violetta Elvin.** Dancers of Today, no. 3. London:
Black, 1953, p. 16.

On the ballerina's performance in **Sylvia.**

6. Movies

*   Braun, Susan, and Jessie Kitching, comps. **Dance and
Mime Film and Videotape Catalog**, p. 18. Cited
above as item 220.

Annotation on a movie version of **Sylvia.**

*   **The Simon and Schuster Book of the Ballet**, pp. 136-
37. Cited above as item 111.

History and plot.

*   **100 [Sto] baletnykh libretto**, pp. 99-105. Cited
above as item 177.

History and plot.

*   Terry, Walter. **Ballet**, pp. 294-97. Cited above as
item 179.

History and plot of **Sylvia** (pages 294-296) and of
Sylvia pas de deux (pages 296-297).

*   _____ . **Ballet Guide**, pp. 330-32. Cited above as
item 180.

History and plot of **Sylvia** (pages 330-332) and of
Sylvia pas de deux (page 332).

*   Vaillat, Léandre. **Ballets de l'Opéra de Paris.** Cited
above as item 112.

This book on the ballets performed at the Paris
Opéra contains some material on **Sylvia.**

*   Verwer, Hans. **Guide to the Ballet**, pp. 50-54, 169-
70. Cited above as item 184.

History and plot.

*   Viveash, Cherry. **Tales from the Ballet**, pp. 15-23.
Cited above as item 185.

History and plot, including a statement that "at
the time the harmonics were considered to be most
unusual."

239. Williams, Peter, John Percival, and Noël Goodwin.
"Sylvia Reduced: Ashton's Sylvia Returns to Covent
Garden in a Single Act." **Dance and Dancers** 19
(February 1968): 20-22.

Very good general article on **Sylvia**, emphasizing
the performance of Frederick Ashton's version. The
section "Musical Remnants" by Goodwin has a perceptive
analysis of the music of the ballet. This and item
232 are perhaps the best general English-language
essays on **Sylvia**, along with Cyril Beaumont's **Complete
Book of Ballets.**

*   Winkler, H.J. **Oper und Ballett,** pp. 373–74. Cited
      above as item 186.

      History and plot.

*   Wolff, Stéphane. **L'Opéra au Palais Garnier, 1875–
      1962,** p. 329. Cited above as item 113.

      Valuable basic data on **Sylvia** as performed at the
      Palais Garnier.

2. Scenarios

240. Barbier, Jules, and Jacques de Reinach. **Sylvia, or,
      The Nymph of Diana: Ballet in Two Acts and Four
      Tableau.** New York: C.D. Koppel, 1886.

241. _____. **Sylvia, ou, La nymphe de Diane: Ballet en
      trois actes, quatre tableaux.** Paris: Calmann
      Lévy, 1876.

3. Music

*   Baldwin, Lillian. **A Listener's Anthology of Music,**
      vol. 2, pp. 403–08. Cited above as item 6.

      Excellent analysis of the music of **Sylvia,** with
      many examples. This and the next item are close rivals
      for the best treatment of the ballet's music.

*   Fiske, Roger. **Ballet Music,** pp. 22, 31–35. Cited
      above as item 195.

      Excellent commentary on the music of **Sylvia,** with
      15 musical themes given. This and the previous item
      are close rivals for the best treatment of the
      ballet's music.

242. "Some Novelties at the Ballet." **Musical Times** 93
      (November 1952): 515.

      Partially a commentary on Frederick Ashton's
      revival of **Sylvia,** but mostly a highly complimentary
      description of Delibes' music. **Sylvia** is called "one
      of the glories of ballet music" and "a treasurable
      musical acquisition to our national ballet."

4. Choreography

*   **Choreography by George Balanchine,** pp. 67–68, 196,
      244–45, 265–67. Cited above as item 118.

      On Balanchine's choreography for **Pizzicato Polka**

(pages 67–68) and S[...]
use of parts of **Sylvi[...]
sement (pages 244–245)[...]
267).

GV 17[...]
O[...]
some[...]
mat[...]

245. Li[...]

*   Vaughan, David. **Frederic[...]
      Cited above as item 204[...]

      Has some material on the[...]
done by Ashton.

5.   Dancers and dance[...] in relation to **Sy**[...]

(The following is a selective [...]
   works on dancers and dance [...]
          contain relevant materi[...]

*   *

*   Benois, Alexander. **Reminiscences of[...]
      Ballet,** pp. 210–18. Cited above as[...]

      On a "catastrophe" in the production[...]   *
(1901), involving Sergei Diaghilev and a[...]
power struggle. The same incident is rel[...]
245.

243. Chujoy, Anatole. **The New York City Ballet.**
      New York: Knopf, 1953.
      GV 1786.N4 C45

      History of the company, with some material on
Sylvia pas de deux.

*   Clarke, Mary. **The Sadler's Wells Ballet.** Cited ab[...]
      as item 207.

      History of the company, with some material on
Sylvia.

*   Franks, Arthur Henry. **Svetlana Beriosova.** Cited
      above as item 210.

      Biography of the ballerina, with material on her
performance in **Sylvia.**

*   Gillard, David. **Beryl Grey.** Cited above as item 211.

      Biography of the ballerina, with material on her
performance in **Sylvia.**

244. Himmel, Paul, and Walter Terry. **Ballet in Action.**
      New York: Putnam, 1954.

7. Derivatives, adaptations, etc.

(See also **Fadetta, Pas de Deux and Divertissement,**
and **Don Parasol**)

248. Joseffy, Rafael. **Pizzicati from "Sylvia" Ballet by
Delibes: Concert Transcription for the Piano.**
New York: G. Schirmer, 1882.

Adaptation of the pizzicati from **Sylvia** into a
piano work.

RADHA

249. Hofmannstahl, Hugo. "Her 'Extraordinary Immediacy'."
Dance Magazine 42 (September 1968): 37-38.

Description of a 1906 performance of **Radha** by
Ruth St. Denis.

250. Martin, John Joseph. "The Dance: 'Radha' Again."
New York Times (July 20, 1941): X9.

On Ruth St. Denis' revival of **Radha.**

251. McDonagh, Don. **The Complete Guide to Modern Dance.**
Garden City, N.Y.: Doubleday, 1976, pp. 28-29.
Citation also used following item 254.
GV 1783.M26   ISBN 0385050550

History and plot.

252. Shelton, Suzanne. **Divine Dancer.** Garden City, N.Y.:
Doubleday, 1981. Citation also used following item
254.
GV 1785.S3 S53   ISBN 0385141599

Biography of Ruth St. Denis, including the scenario
of **Radha** and commentary on the ballet.

253. Terry, Walter. **Miss Ruth: The 'More Living Life' of
Ruth St. Denis.** New York: Dodd, Mead, 1969.
Citation also used following item 254.
GV 1785.S3 T4

Biography of the ballerina, with much material on
Radha.

254. ———— . "Return of Radha." **New York Herald Tribune**
(July 6, 1941).

On Ruth St. Denis' revival of **Radha.**

COBRAS

*   McDonagh, Don. **The Complete Guide to Modern Dance,**
       p. 27. Cited above as item 251.

       History and plot.

*   Shelton, Suzanne. **Divine Dancer.** Cited above as item
       252.

       Biography of Ruth St. Denis, including some
       material on **Cobras.**

*   Terry, Walter. **Miss Ruth.** Cited above as item 253.

       Biography of Ruth St. Denis, with some material on
       Cobras.

KARNAVAL

255. Krasovskaĭa, Vera Milhaĭlovna. **Russkiĭ baletnyĭ teatr
       nachala XX veka.** Leningrad: Iskusstvo, 1971–72,
       vol. 1, pp. 277–83.
       GV 1787.K688

       Has some material on **Karnaval.**

SOIR DE FÊTE

256. Anderson, Jack. "Springtime in France: A Traveller's
       Report." **Dance Magazine** 49 (July 1975):   32.

       Brief history and description of **Soir de fête,**
       and commentary on a French performance of the ballet.

257. Christout, Marie Françoise. "New Ballet and a Revival
       at the Paris Opéra." **Dance and Dancers** 7 (October
       1956):   26–27.

       Contains a commentary on a revival of **Soir de
       fête.**

258. Dumesnil, René. "La danse à l'Opéra de Paris depuis
       1900." **L'art du ballet des origines à nos jours.**
       Paris: Editions du tambourinaire, 1952, p. 148.

       On the history of **Soir de fête.**

259. Percival, John. "The Opéra Renewed." **Dance and
       Dancers** 25 (July 1974);   34–35.

       On the history of **Soir de fête** and its revival

in Paris. The historical impact of the ballet is well summarized in the statement, "Of all the ballets created for the Paris Opéra in the present century, **Soir de fête** has been the most consistently popular over the years."

*   Wolff, Stéphane. **L'Opéra au Palais Garnier, 1875– 1962**, p. 325. Cited above as item 113.

Valuable basic data on **Soir de fête** as performed at the Palais Garnier.

STAGEFRIGHT

260. DeMille, Agnes. "Début at the Opera." **Dance Magazine** 2 (April 1928): 32–33.

On the performance of **Stagefright**.

FADETTA

261. Leningrad. Malyĭ opernyĭ teatr. **Fadetta: Balet v 3 deistviiakh, muzyka Leo Deliba.** Leningrad: ONTI im. Evg. Sokolovoĭ, 1936.

Scenario.

FLOURESCENCES

*   Wolff, Stéphane. **L'Opéra au Palais Garnier, 1875– 1962**, p. 281. Cited above as item 113.

Valuable basic data on **Flourescences** as performed at the Palais Garnier.

PIÈCE D'OCCASION

262. Clarke, Mary. "Festival Activities." **Dancing Times,** no. 589 (October 1959): 16.

Brief material on the initial production of **Pièce d'occasion.**

PAS DE DEUX AND DIVERTISSEMENT

*   **Choreography by George Balanchine,** pp. 244–45. Cited above as item 118.

On Balanchine's choreography for **Pas de Deux and Divertissement.**

263. Hering, Doris. "New York City Ballet, Three Pre-
          mieres: 'Pas de Deux and Divertissement'
          (Jan. 14)..." **Dance Magazine** 39 (March 1965):
          67–68.

      On the initial production of **Pas de Deux and
      Divertissement.**

*   Reynolds, Nancy. **Repertory in Review,** p. 230. Cited
          above as item 120.

      On the New York City Ballet's performance of **Pas de
      Deux and Divertissement.**

                          CELEBRATION

*   Balanchine, George, and Francis Mason. **Balanchine's
          Complete Stories of the Great Ballets,** pp. 99–101.
          Cited above as item 102.

      History and plot.

*   _____ . **101 Stories of Great Ballets,** pp. 46–48.
          Cited above as item 126.

      History and plot.

                       LE JARDIN ANIMÉ

264. Anderson, Jack. "New York Newsletter." **Dancing
          Times,** no. 850 (July 1982):   686–87.

      Includes brief material on the performance of **Le
      jardin animé.**

265. Goldner, Nancy. "American Ballet Theatre, Petipa
          Program, Metropolitan Opera House, Apr. 20–June 13."
          Dance News 47 (September 1981):   13.

      Includes commentary on the performance of **Le jardin
      animé.**

                         DON PARASOL

266. Fritzsche, Dietmar. "Ballet-Premiere 'Don Parasol'
          an der Komischen Oper Berlin." **Musik und Gesell-
          schaft** 31 (October 1981):   627–29.

      On the initial production of **Don Parasol.**

DELIBES' OPERAS IN GENERAL

267. Clément, Félix, and Pierre Larousse. **Dictionnaire
     des opéras (Dictionnaire lyrique).** Revised by
     Arthur Pougin. Paris: Librairie Larousse, 1905.
     ML 102.06 C42

     Contains short articles on several of Delibes'
     operas. Other editions were published in 1881, 1897,
     and 1969.

268. Hughes, Gervase. **Composers of Operetta.** London:
     Macmillan, 1962, pp. 55-58.
     ML 390.H887 C59

     Very good overview of Delibes' light operas, with
     musical examples. Another edition was published in
     1962 by St. Martin's, New York.

269. Loewenberg, Alfred, comp. **Annals of Opera, 1597-1940.**
     3d ed. Totowa, N.J.: Rowman and Littlefield, 1978.
     ML 102.06 L6 1978   ISBN 0874718511

     Outstanding reference book on opera, with a
     detailed record of productions as well as other his-
     torical data. Four of Delibes' operas are included.
     Other editions were published in 1943, 1955, and 1970.

270. Traubner, Richard. **Operetta: A Theatrical History.**
     Garden City, N.Y.: Doubleday, 1983, pp. 97-98.
     Citation also used following item 276.
     ML 1900.T7   ISBN 0385132328

     Fine short article on Delibes' contribution to
     operetta.

271. Walsh, T.J. **Second Empire Opera: The Théâtre
     Lyrique, Paris, 1851-1870.** London: J. Calder,
     1981.
     ML 1727.8.P2 W3 1981   ISBN 0714536598

     Valuable data on Delibes' operas of the period, in-
     cluding a chronology of the theater's repertory and an
     index by composer of the operas performed at the
     theater.

INDIVIDUAL OPERAS

SIX DEMOISELLES À MARIER

272. Jaime, E., and Adolphe Choler. **Six Demoiselles à Marier: Opérette bouffe en un acte.** Paris: M. Lévy Frères, 1857.

Libretto; Jaime's name was left off the libretto.

MAÎTRE GRIFFARD

273. Soubies, Albert. **Histoire du Théâtre—Lyrique, 1851— 1870.** Paris: Fischbacher, 1899. Citation also used following item 274.
ML 1727.8.P2 S7

Has some data on **Maître Griffard.**

LE JARDINIER ET SON SEIGNEUR

274. Carré, Michel, and Théodore Barrière. **Le jardinier et son seigneur: Opéra comique en un acte.** Paris: M. Lévy Frères, 1863.

Libretto; Carré's name was left off the libretto.

*   Soubies, Albert. **Histoire du Théâtre—Lyrique, 1851— 1870.** Cited above as item 273.

Has some data on **Le jardinier et son seigneur.**

LE SERPENT À PLUMES

275. Loppert, Max. "On Radio." **Opera** 24 (November 1973): 1039—40.

On a radio performance of **Le serpent à plumes.** Delibes' music is thought of very highly by Loppert.

MALBROUGH S'EN VA-T-EN GUERRE

*   Curtiss, Mina. **Bizet and His World,** pp. 207—09. Cited above as item 15.

Amusing section on the composition of **Marlbrough s'en va-t-en guerre,** including the translation of a letter from Delibes explaining the authorship of the work.

L'ÉCOSSAIS DE CHATOU

276. Reyer, Ernest. "L'écossais de Chatou." **Journal des débats** (November 16, 1879).

Contemporary commentary on **L'écossais de Chatou.**

*   Traubner, Richard. **Operetta**, p. 98. Cited above as item 270.

Unflattering description and short plot.

LE COUR DU ROI PÉTAUD

277. Jaime, Adolphe, and Philippe Gille. **Le cour du roi Pétaud: Opéra bouffe en trois actes.** Paris: M. Lévy Frères, 1869.

Libretto.

LE ROI L'A DIT

278. Asche, Gerhart. "Warten auf das Original: Delibes' der König hat's gesagt in Hildesheim." **Opernwelt** 24, no. 5 (1983): 43.

On the performance of **Le roi l'a dit** in Hildesheim.

*   Bethléem, L. [and others]. **Les opéras, les opéras-comiques, et les opérettes**, p. 144. Cited above as item 129.

History and plot.

279. Beuth, Reinhard. "Bonn." **Opernwelt** (August 1969): 40.

On the performance of **Le roi l'a dit** in Bonn.

280. Bury, H. Blaze de. "Le roi l'a dit." **Revue de deux mondes** (June 1, 1873).

On the original production of **Le roi l'a dit.**

281. Dannenberg, Peter. "Hannover: Belle epoque." **Opernwelt** (June 1971): 28–29.

On the performance of **Le roi l'a dit** in Hannover.

282. Drone, Jeanette Marie. **Index to Opera, Operetta and Musical Comedy Synopses in Collections and**

Periodicals. Metuchen, N.J.: Scarecrow Press, 1978.
Citation also used following item 312.
ML 128.04 D76   ISBN 0810811006

Indexes publications which have plots of **Le roi
l'a dit.** Some of the sources indexed are included in
this bibliography.

283. Eckstein, Paul. "Liberec." **Opera** 16 (March 1965):
     185.

     On the performance of **Le roi l'a dit** in
     Czechoslovakia.

284. Ewen, David. **The Book of European Light Opera.**
     New York: Holt, Rinehart and Winston, 1962,
     pp. 206–07.
     MT 95.E9

     Plot and mention of the more important songs.

285. ―――― . **The New Encyclopedia of the Opera.** New York:
     Hill and Wang, 1971, p. 590. Citation also used
     following item 314.
     ML 102.06 E9 1971   ISBN 0809072629

     History and plot.

286. Gille, Phillipe. "Le roi l'a dit." **Le Théâtre,** no. 4
     (April 1898).

     On Gille's two act revival of **Le roi l'a dit** in
     1898.

287. Hartmann, Ludwig. **Der König hat's gesagt (Le roi l'a
     dit): Komische Oper.** Leipzig: Seeman, 1901.

     Criticism of **Le roi l'a dit.** This is the most
     substantial work on the opera.

288. Hughes, Gervase. **Sidelights on a Century of Music,
     1825–1924.** London: Macdonald, 1969, pp. 120–24.
     ML 196.H83   ISBN 0356028334

     Best English language essay on **Le roi l'a dit,**
     preceded by an excellent general essay on Delibes
     (pages 116–20). Another edition was published in
     1970 by St. Martins, New York.

289. Kalbeck, Max. **Opern-Abende: Beitrage zur Geschichte
     und Kritik der Oper.** Berlin: Harmonie, 1883,

vol. 2, pp. 119–26.

Essay on **Le roi l'a dit**.

290. **Knoch's Opera Guide: Contains Over Two Hundred Descriptions of Celebrated Operas with Short Biographies of Their Composers.** Vienna: R. Lechner, [1927], pp. 438–40. Citation also used following item 321.

Plot.

291. Melitz, Leo. **The Opera Goer's Complete Guide: Comprising Two Hundred and Nine Opera Plots with Musical Numbers and Casts.** Translated by Richard Salinger. New York: Dodd, Mead, 1908, `. pp. 207–08. Citation also used following item 326. MT 95.M3

Plot.

292. "Opera and Ballet in London." **Musical Opinion** 89 (September 1966): 717.

On the performance of **Le roi l'a dit** in London.

293. Reyer, Ernest. "Le roi l'a dit." **Journal des débats** (May 29, 1873, July 6, 1885).

Contemporary commentary on **Le roi l'a dit**.

294. Schmidt-Garre, Helmut. "München: 'Der König hat's gesagt': Wiederentdeckte Oper von Delibes." **Neue Zeitschrift für Musik** 126 (October 1965): 393–94.

On the performance of **Le roi l'a dit** in Munich.

295. **The Simon and Schuster Book of the Opera: A Complete Reference Guide, 1597 to the Present.** New York: Simon and Schuster, 1977, pp. 259. Citation also used following item 336. ML 102.06 063   ISBN 0671248863

History and plot; translation of **L'opera: Répertorio della lirica dal 1597.**

296. Soubies, Albert, and Charles Malherbe. **Histoire de L'Opéra Comique: La second Salle Favart, 1840–1887.** 2 vols. Paris: Librairie Marpon et Flammarion, 1892–93. Citation also used following

items 304 and 336.
ML 1727.8.P2   S73

Volume 2 has some good historical material on **Le roi l'a dit.**

297. ———— . **Histoire de l'Opéra Comique: La second Salle Favart, 1840–1887.** 2 vols. Geneva: Minkoff reprint, 1978. Citation also used following items 304 and 336.
ML 1727.8.P2   S73   1978   ISBN 2826606298

Reprint of item 296.

298. Steyer, Rolf. "Munich." **Opera** 16 (November 1965): 829–30.

On the performance of **Le roi l'a dit** in Munich.

299. Strantz, Ferdinand von, and Adolf Stauch. **Der grosse Opernführer.** Munich: E. Vollmer, 1978, pp. 90–92. Citation also used following item 336.
MT 95.S895 1978   ISBN 3878760418

History and plot.

300. Wolff, Stéphane. "Le roi l'a dit." **Opera** 10 (June 1959):   379–80.

On the performance of **Le roi l'a dit** in Bordeaux.

JEAN DE NIVELLE

*   Bethléem, L. [and others]. **Les opéras, les opéras-comiques, et les opérettes,** pp. 145–46. Cited above as item 129.

History and plot.

*   Boston, Margie Viola. "An Essay on the Life and Works of Leo Delibes," leaves 33–38, 78–79. Cited above as item 10.

History of **Jean de Nivelle** (leaves 33–38), and plot (leaves 78–79). This is perhaps the best work on the opera.

301. Bury, H. Blaze de. "Jean de Nivelle." **Revue de deux mondes** (October 15 1880).

On the original production of **Jean de Nivelle.**

302. Décé, H. "Jean de Nivelle à la Gaîté Lyrique." **Le théâtre,** no. 238 (November 1908).

On the revival of **Jean de Nivelle** in Paris.

303. Hanslick, Eduard. **Aus dem Opernleben der Gegenwart.**
     Berlin: Allegemeiner Verein für Deutsche
     Literatur, 1885, pp. 57-66.

     Contemporary commentary on **Jean de Nivelle.**

*   Jullien, Adolphe. **Musiciens d'aujourd'hui,** pp. 266-
      75. Cited above as item 235.

      Interesting history of and commentary on **Jean de
      Nivelle.**

304. Reyer, Ernest. "Jean de Nivelle." **Journal des débats**
     (March 14, 1880): 107-09.

     Contemporary commentary on **Jean de Nivelle.**

*   Soubies, Albert, and Charles Malherbe. **Histoire de
      l'Opéra Comique.** Cited above as item 297.

      Volume 2 has some good historical material on
      Jean de Nivelle.

LAKMÉ

1. History, plots, other general works

   (The history and plot materials below,
   which vary in content, were selected from
   a wide body of material)

*   Bethléem, L. [and others]. **Les opéras, les opéras-
      comique, et les opérettes,** pp. 146-47. Cited
      above as item 129.

      History and plot.

305. Biancolli, Louis, ed. **The Opera Reader.** New York:
     McGraw-Hill, 1953, pp. 115-19.
     ML 1700.B47

     Very good material on **Lakmé,** giving the plot,
     history and importance of the opera, along with some
     material on Delibes in general. Another edition was
     published in 1953 by Grosset & Dunlap, New York.

306. Biancolli, Louis, and Robert Bagar, eds. **The Victor
     Book of Operas.** Newly rev. ed. New York: Simon
     and Schuster, 1953, pp. 240-44.
     MT 150.V4 1953

     History and plot.

*   Boston, Margie Viola. "An Essay on the Life and Works
        of Leo Delibes," leaves 41-50. Cited above as item
        10.

        History of **Lakmé**.

307.   Bulla, Clyde Robert. **More Stories of Favorite Operas.**
        New York: Crowell, 1965, pp. 182-91.
        MT 95.B936

        Plot.

308.   Bury, H. Blaze de. "M. Léo Delibes et Lakmé. . ."
        Revue de deux mondes (July 15, 1883).

        On the original production of **Lakmé**.

309.   **Composers' Autographs: Volume 2, From Schubert to
        Stravinsky.** Madison [N.J.]: Fairleigh Dickinson
        University Press, 1968, pp. 54, 170.

        Page 54 is a reproduction of a manuscript of **Lakmé**,
        and page 170 is a description of the manuscript.
        Another edition was published in 1968 by Cassell,
        London.

310.   Cross, Milton. **Milton Cross' Complete Stories of the
        Great Operas.** Garden City. N.Y.: Doubleday, 1947,
        pp. 289-95.
        MT 95.C76

        History and plot. Another edition was published in
        1952.

311.   Davidson, Gladys. **Standard Stories from the Operas.**
        London: W. Lauries, 1944, pp. 131-37, 954.

        Plot (pages 131-137), plus list of three produc-
        tions (page 954). Other editions were published.

312.   DelBonta, Robert J. "Songs of India." **Opera
        Quarterly** 2, no. 1 (1984): 5-14.

        On the influence of India on western musical works,
        including **Lakmé**.

*   Drone, Jeanette Marie. **Index to Opera, Operetta and
        Musical Comedy Synopses in Collections and Periodi-
        cals.** Cited above as item 282.

        Indexes publications which have plots of **Lakmé**.
        Some of the sources indexed are included in this

bibliography.

313. Eaton, Quaintance. **Opera: A Pictorial Guide.** New
         York: Abaris Books, 1980, pp. 70-71.
      MT 95.E2   ISBN 0913870714

         History and plot.

314. ———— . **Opera Production: A Handbook.** Minneapolis:
         University of Minnesota Press, 1961, pp. 85-86.
      MT 955.E25   ISBN 0816606897

         Plot, plus requirements for production of the opera.

*   Ewen, David. **The Complete Book of Classical Music,**
         pp. 655-57. Cited above as item 145.

         History and plot. A short general essay on Delibes
      is on pages 652-653.

*   ———— . **The Encyclopedia of Musical Masterpieces,**
         pp. 180-81. Cited above as item 146.

         Well-written reference article.

*   ———— . **Ewen's Musical Masterworks,** pp. 198-99.
         Cited above as item 147.

         Well-written reference article.

*   ———— . **The New Encyclopedia of the Opera,**
         pp. 360-61. Cited above as item 285.

         History and plot.

315. Fassett, Stephen. "Bell Song from Lakme". **Hobbies**
         49 (April 1944): 25.

         Short but knowledgable article on the bell song.
      It tells how Delibes composed the music with Marie Van
      Zandt, an American soprano who sang the title role in
      the initial production of **Lakmé,** in mind. Also, the
      voice requirements for the song are described:
      "sopranos with high, agile voices." Most of the
      article is dedicated to the history and criticism of
      recordings of the opera.

316. Fuld, James J. **The Book of World-Famous Libretti:
         The Musical Theater from 1598 to Today.** New York:
         Pendragon Press, 1984, pp. 162-63.
      ML 128.04 F8 1984   ISBN 0918728274

Data on the libretto of **Lakmé,** plus a facsimile of
its cover.

*   _____ . **The Book of World-Famous Music,** pp. 120–21.
Cited above as item 233.

On the bell song.

317. Harewood, George, ed. **Kobbé's Complete Opera Book.**
New York: Putnam, 1972, pp. 791–96.
MT 95.K52 1972   ISBN 0399110445

History, plot, and three musical themes. For a
similar edition, see the 1954 edition published by
Putnam, New York.

318. _____ . **Kobbé's Complete Opera Book.** London:
Putnam, 1976, pp. 821–26.
MT 95.K52 1976b   ISBN 0370100204

History, plot, and three musical themes; same as
item 319.

319. _____ . **The New Kobbé's Complete Opera Book.** New
York: Putnam, 1976, pp. 821–26.
MT 95.K52 1976   ISBN 0399116338

History, plot, and three musical themes; same as
item 318.

320. Howard, John Tasker. **The World's Great Operas.**
New York: Random House, 1948, pp. 195–96.
MT 95.H68

Plot. Another edition was published in 1948 by
Grosset & Dunlap, New York.

*   Jullien, Adolphe. **Musiciens d'aujourd'hui,** pp. 275–
82. Cited above as item 235.

Interesting history of and commentary on **Lakmé.**

321. Kerst, Leon. "Lakmé." **Revue du monde musical et
dramatique** 6 (April 21, 1883): 244–49.

On the original production of **Lakmé.**

*   **Knoch's Opera Guide,** pp. 282–83. Cited above as
item 290.

Plot.

322. Kobbé, Gustav. **The Complete Opera Book: The Stories of the Operas, Together with 400 of the Leading Airs and Motives in Musical Notation.** New York: Putnam, 1922, pp. 724–25.
     MT 95.K52 1922

     History and plot.

323. Kohrs, Karl, ed. **The New Milton Cross' Complete Stories of the Great Operas.** Rev. and enlarged ed. Garden City, N.Y.: Doubleday, 1955, pp. 303–309.

     History and plot.

324. Krehbiel, Henry Edward. **A Second Book of Operas.** Garden City, N.Y.: Garden City Publishing Co., 1917, pp. 95–103.

     In-depth analysis of **Lakmé** and its music. Another edition was published in 1917 by Macmillan, New York.

325. Loisel, Joseph. **Lakmé de Léo Delibes: Étude historique et critique, analyse musicale.** Paris: P. Mellottée, 1924. 218 p.

     Most important work on **Lakmé,** giving: a brief life of Delibes; the history of **Lakmé**'s composition; press criticism of the premiere; the success of the opera; its interpreters; and its plot. Most of the book is dedicated to musical analysis, with 133 musical examples offered. The book ends with a brief conclusion strongly supporting the music of Delibes.

326. McSpadden, John Walker. **Operas and Musical Comedies.** Enlarged ed. New York: Crowell, 1951, pp. 245–47.
     MT 95.M154 1951

     History, plot, and two musical themes.

*   Melitz, Leo. **The Opera Goer's Complete Guide,** pp. 187–88. Cited above as item 291.

     Plot.

327. Mendelsohn, Felix. **The Story of A Hundred Operas.** New York: Grosset & Dunlap, 1940, pp. 147–49.
     MT 95.M47 1940

     Plot. Other editions were published in 1913 and 1923.

328. Miller, Philip Lieson. "The Orientalism of Lakmé."
      Opera News 6 (December 22, 1941): 18-21.

      Very good article on the oriental flavor of **Lakmé**.
      He claims that most representations of the Orient in
      western music are far from genuine, and using **Lakmé**
      as a prime example, states: "a composer of Delibes'
      time could express the spirit of the Orient in terms
      which his compatriots could understand (even though
      true orientals could not)" and "we must concentrate
      on intention rather than effect." Same essay as item
      329.

329. _____ . "The Orientalism of Lakmé." **Opera Lover's
      Companion.** Edited by Mary Ellis Peltz. Chicago:
      Ziff-Davis, 1948, pp. 125-28.
      MT 95.P48

      Same essay as item 328. Preceding it is an essay
      on the history of **Lakmé** (item 333).

330. Moore, Frank Ledlie, comp. **Crowell's Handbook of
      World Opera.** New York: Crowell, 1961, pp. 89-90.
      ML 102.06 M6

      History, plot, and mention of the most important
      songs.

331. Newman, Ernest. **More Stories of Famous Operas.** New
      York: Knopf, 1943, pp. 159-77.

      MT 95.N5 M6

      One of the best reference pieces on **Lakmé,**
      including history, plot, and musical themes.

332. Peltz, Mary Ellis, and Robert Lawrence. **The Metro-
      politan Opera Guide.** New York: Modern Library,
      1939, pp. 307-13.
      MT 95.P46 M3

      History, plot, and musical themes, with a well-
      expressed statement of Delibes' contribution to opera:
      "a natural gift of melodiousness and vivacity
      developed with an elegance and polish that he achieved
      from constant practical experimentation." Other edi-
      tions were also published.

333. Peyser, Herbert F. "Lakme." **Opera Lover's Companion.**
      Edited by Mary Ellis Peltz. Chicago: Ziff-Davis,
      1948, pp. 121-25.

MT 95.P48

> Very good essay on the history of **Lakmé**. Following it is an essay on the orientalism of **Lakmé** (item 329).

334. Reyer, Ernest. "Lakmé." **Journal des débats** (April 22, 1883, May 16, 1884, October 17, 1884).

> Contemporary commentary on **Lakmé**.

* Rohozinski, Ladislas, ed. **Cinquante ans de musique française, de 1874 à 1925**, vol. 1, pp. 134–35. Cited above as item 52.

> Good material on the history of **Lakmé**, including one illustration of a stage setting.

* Sharp, Stuart Walter. "The Twilight of French Opéra Lyrique, 1880–1900," leaves 162–222. Cited above as item 54.

> Best English work on **Lakmé**, with: a brief history; a synopsis of the libretto; and an excellent extended analysis of the music containing 40 musical examples.

335. Simon, Henry W. **Festival of Opera**. Garden City N.Y.: Hanover House, 1957, pp. 281–85.
MT 95.S59

> Well-done history and plot. Another edition was published in 1957 by W.H. Allen, London.

336. Simon, Henry W., ed. **The Victor Book of the Opera.** 13th ed. New York: Simon and Schuster, 1968, pp. 206–08.
MT 150.V4 1968

> Well-done history and plot.

* **The Simon and Schuster Book of the Opera**, pp. 285–86, 292. Cited above as item 295.

> History and plot (pages 285–286), and facsimile of a poster (page 292).

* Soubies, Albert, and Charles Malherbe. **Histoire de l'Opéra Comique.** Cited above as item 296.

> Volume 2 has some good historical material on **Lakmé**.

* _____ . **Histoire de l'Opéra Comique.** Cited above as

item 297.

Reprint of previous item.

*   Strantz, Ferdinand von, and Adolf Stauch. **Der grosse Opernführer**, pp. 92-93. Cited above as item 299.

History and plot.

337.   Thompson, Oscar. **Plots of the Operas: 266 Stories of the Operas.** Cleveland: World Publishing Co., 1943, pp. 259-60.
MT 95.T54 P6 1943

History and plot. Other editions were published.

338.   Upton, George P. **The Standard Light Operas: Their Plots and Their Music: A Handbook.** Chicago: A.C. McClurg, 1902, pp. 70-72.
MT 95.U70

Plot and analysis of the music.

339.   ———— . **The Standard Operas: Their Plots and Their Music.** Chicago: A.C. McClurg, 1925, pp. 69-71.
MT 95.U74

Plot and analysis of the music.

340.   Upton, George P., and Felix Borowski. **The Standard Opera Guide.** Garden City, N.Y.: Halcyon House, 1947, pp. 67-69.
MT 95.U75 1947

History and plot. Another edition was published in 1940 by Blue Ribbon Books, New York.

341.   **The Victor Book of the Opera: Stories of the Operas with Illustrations and Descriptions of Victor Opera Records.** 10th ed. Camden, N.J.: RCA Manufacturing Co., 1936, pp. 212-15.
MT 150.R697 1936

History and plot.

342.   **The Victrola Book of the Opera: Stories of the Operas with Illustrations & Descriptions of** :tor **Victor Opera Records.** 6th ed. Camden, N.J.: Victor Talking Machine Co., 1921, pp. 175-79.

History and plot.

343. Wagnalls, Mabel. **Stars of the Opera.** Rev. and
          enlarged ed. New York: Funk & Wagnalls, 1909,
          pp. 315-36.

      Mostly an extended story of the opera, but a
      description and analysis of the music is intermingled
      with the unfolding of the plot. This is perhaps the
      most interesting description of the opera. Other
      editions were published in 1899 and 1907 under this
      title, and in 1924 and 1929 under the title: **Opera
      and Its Stars.**

344. Winternitz, Emanuel. **Musical Autographs from
          Monteverdi to Hindemith.** New York: Dover, 1965,
          plate 140, page 115.
      ML 96.4.W5 1965

      Reproduction of the manuscript for the opening bars
      of the bell song (plate 140) and a description of the
      manuscript (page 115). Another edition was published
      in 1955 by Princeton University Press.

2. Librettos

345. Gondinet, Edmond, and Philippe Gille. **Lakmé: Opéra
          en trois actes.** Paris: Calman Lévy, 1884.

346. ———— . **Lakmé: Opera in Three Acts.** Boston:
          O. Ditson, 1890.

      English and Italian libretto.

3. Derivatives, adaptations, etc.

      (See also the derived ballets **Radha,
          Cobras** and **Pipes of Pan**)

*   **Choreography by George Balanchine,** pp. 76, 101, 124.
      Cited above as item 118.

      On a ballet created by Balanchine from act two of
      Lakmé.

KASSYA

347. Bellaigue, Camille. "Kassya." **Revue de deux mondes**
          (April 1, 1893).

      On the original production of **Kassya.**

*   Bethléem, L. [and others]. **Les opéras, les opéras**

comiques, et les opérettes, p. 148. Cited above as
item 129.

History and plot.

*   Boston, Margie Viola. "An Essay on the Life and Works
    of Leo Delibes, leaves 50–58, 79–80. Cited above
    as item 10.

History of Kassya (leaves 50–58) and plot (leaves
79–80). This is perhaps the best work on **Kassya.**

*   Harding, James. **Massenet,** pp. 107–08. Cited above as
    item 29.

On Massenet's completion of Kassya after Delibes'
death.

*   Jullien, Adolphe. **Musiciens d'aujourd'hui,** pp. 282–
    89. Cited above as item 235.

Interesting history and commentary on **Kassya.**

348. Moreno, H. "Kassya." **Le ménestrel** 59 (March 24,
    1893): 97–98

On the original production of **Kassya,**
including a brief discussion of the manuscript score.

DELIBES' SONGS

349. Noske, Frits. **French Song from Berlioz to Duparc:**
    The Origin and Development of the Mélodie. 2d ed.,
    revised by Rita Benson and Frits Noske. Translated
    by Rita Benson. New York: Dover, 1970, pp. 203–
    10.
ML 2827.N613 1970   ISBN 0486221040

Excellent material on Delibes' songs, with nine
musical examples. Translation and revision of **La
mélodie française de Berlioz à Duparc.**

*   Rohozinski, Ladislas, ed. **Cinquante ans de musique
    française, de 1874 à 1925,** vol. 2. p. 6. Cited
    above as item 52.

Facsimile of a manuscript of the mélodie **Myrto.**

350. Spills, Helen. "French Art–Song Composers before
    Fauré and Debussy: Berlioz, Bizet, Delibes."
    Etude 62 (January 1944): 19, 52.

Contains brief material on Delibes' songs in
general.

OTHER WORKS

LA MORT D'ORPHÉE

*   Jullien, Adolphe. **Musiciens d'aujourd'hui**, p. 269.
Cited above as item 235.

Facsimile of letter by Delibes concerning **La mort
d'Orphée.**

351.   Reyer, Ernest. "La morte d'Orphée." **Journal des
débats** (March 30, 1885).

Contemporary commentary on **La mort d'Orphée.**

LE CHANT DES LAVANDIÈRES

352.   Reyer, Ernest. "Chanson des Lavandières." **Journal
des débats** (April 13, 1879).

Contemporary commentary on **Le chant des
Lavandières.**

GENERAL INFORMATION

RESEARCH LACUNAE

Several areas relating to Delibes are in need of further research and publication. First, there is no full bio- graphy of Delibes in English, although Margie Boston's 1981 thesis on Delibes is a very good start in this direction. Second, the controversy over whether Tchaikovsky modelled his ballets on Delibes' should be more completely resolved if possible. Third, a substantial and comprehensive work on **Sylvia** is definitely needed. Fourth, his lesser-known works (that is, the works other than **Coppélia, Sylvia**, and **Lakmé**) should be more adequately researched. Among the possible topics are: the confusion between **La source** (also called **Naïla**) and **Valse, ou, Pas de fleurs** (subsequently called the **Naïla Waltz** because of its later insertion into **La source**); a complete history and analysis of **La source**, from which at least four other ballets have derived music; and whether **Kassya** would have had a more favorable fate if Delibes had completed it rather than Massenet.

LIBRARY RESOURCES FOR RESEARCH

Three collections contain significant material for research on Delibes. One is the New York Public Library's magnifi- cent comprehensive dance collection which has a large amount of books, periodicals, films, illustrations, clippings, ephemera, etc. on Delibes' ballets and on Delibes in general. The other two are the fine resources of the Dé- partement de la Musique, Bibliothèque nationale, Paris, and of the Bibliothèque de l'Opéra, Paris.

PERSONAL NAME DICTIONARY

Adam, Adolphe (1803-1856): prominent French composer of operas and ballets who was the principal teacher, mentor, and probably a substitute father for Delibes, and who prob- ably was the key influence on Delibes' talent for ballet. Delibes made a vocal-piano score of Adam's opéra comique **À Clichy** (published in 1855), and arranged a "Polka brillante" in 1856 from Adam's opéra comique **Falstaff.**

Aminta (or Amyntas): principal male character in **Sylvia.**
He is a young shepherd in love with Sylvia. At first Sylvia
rejects him but ultimately after a series of events in a
mythological context the couple are happily united in love.

Barbier, Jules (1822-1901): very successful French
librettist who was the author, with Baron Jacques de
Reinach, of the scenario for **Sylvia.**

Bizet, Georges (1838-1875): well-known composer whose most
successful work was the opera **Carmen.** Delibes and Bizet
admired each other's music, and collaborated on the 1867
operatic work **Marlbrough s'en va-t-en guerre,** but were not
particularly close on a personal basis. Their music has
some definite similarities.

Bozzacchi, Guiseppina (1853-1870): Italian ballerina who
created the role of Swanilda in **Coppélia,** but who died of a
fever on her 17th birthday after dancing in only 18 performances of the ballet.

Coppélia: beautiful life-like mechanical doll in the ballet
of that name, built by Doctor Coppelius. The doll is
believed to be the daughter of Coppelius, and attracts the
love-interest of Franz, and the jealousy of Franz's fiancée,
Swanilda. After the "girl with the enamel eyes" is dis-
covered to be an automaton, the two young lovers are united
in marriage.

Coppelius, Doctor: character in **Coppélia.** He is an
eccentric and misanthropic toymaker and magician who created
the doll Coppélia, which he loved as if she were a living
daughter.

Delibes, Clémence Batiste: mother of Delibes, 27 years old
at the birth of her son. From a Parisian musical family
which included her father, a baritone at the Opéra-Comique,
and her brother Édouard, an organist and professor at the
Paris Conservatory, she was an excellent musician who taught
Léo the fundamentals of music and possibly more. Apparently, she was a strong positive influence on his early
development.

Delibes, Léontine Estelle Mesnage (called Denain): wife of
Delibes and daughter of the well-known French comedienne
Madame Pauline Denain. Léo and Léontine married in 1872.

Diana: goddess of the moon and the hunt, and a character in
Sylvia. She is the dominant force in the sacred woods, and
Sylvia is one of her nymphs. Diana is angry at Sylvia and
Aminta for their part in all the confusion that evolves, but
in the end forgives the lovers.

Eros: god of love, and a character in **Sylvia**. He is very instrumental in the successful union of the lovers Sylvia and Aminta. Originally, the role was played by a ballerina in travesty.

Franz: principal male character in **Coppélia**. He is the fiancé of Swanilda but is in love with Coppélia, a life-like mechanical doll. After he discovers that Coppélia is only a doll, he is reunited with Swanilda, and they marry. Originally, the role was danced by a ballerina in travesty.

Gérald: principal male character in **Lakmé**. He is a British officer stationed in India who falls in love with Lakmé, the daughter of a Brahmin.

Gille, Philippe (1831-1901): close friend of Delibes and librettist or co-librettist for eight of Delibes' operatic works, including **Jean de Nivelle, Lakmé,** and **Kassya.** He also modified **Le roi l'a dit** into two acts for a 1898 production and wrote the lyrics for eight of Delibes' choruses and one of his mélodies.

Gondinet, Edmond (1828-1888): librettist for **Le roi l'a dit** and co-librettist with Philippe Gille for **Jean de Nivelle** and **Lakmé.**

Hervé (1825-1892): pseudonym of Florimond Ronger, minor French composer. He was the proprietor of the Folies-Nouvelles in Paris, and the primary source of its repertory. Because Hervé decided to bring some fresh outside material into his theater, Delibes, who was the accompanist at the Théâtre-Lyrique across the street, got a chance to be a composer and produced his first work, **Deux sous de charbon,** at Hervé's theater.

Hoffmann, Ernst Theodor Amadeus (1776-1822): famous German writer whose story **Der Sandmann** was the source of the plot for **Coppélia.**

Lakmé: principal female character in the opera of the same name. She is the daughter of the Brahmin priest Nilakantha who vows to kill the British officer Gérald with whom Lakmé is in love. In the end, when Lakmé realizes that Gérald is having difficulty deciding between his duty and his love for her, she commits suicide thus making the choice for him.

Massenet, Jules (1842-1912): noted French composer and friend of Delibes. He completed Delibes' almost-finished opera **Kassya** in 1893.

Mérante, Louis (1828-1887): French dancer and choreographer who had leading dance roles in the original productions of

La source and **Sylvia,** was the choreographer for **Sylvia,** and
possibly also collaborated on the scenario for **Sylvia.**

Minkus, Léon (1827-1890): Austrian-born composer whose
original name was Aloisius Ludwig Minkus. He collaborated
with Delibes on **La source,** composing scenes 1 and 4, while
Delibes wrote scenes 2 and 3.

Naïla: principal character in **La source.** She is the
spirit of a spring in a fictitious Persia.

Nilakantha: character in **Lakmé.** He is an Indian Brahmin
priest who is the father of Lakmé. Because the English
officer Gérald has violated the sacred ground of the
Brahmin's temple, he vows to kill the Englishman. When
Lakmé commits suicide at the end, Nilakantha's anger
dissipates.

Nuitter, Charles (1828-1899): pseudonym of Charles Truinet
who with Arthur Saint-Léon was co-scenarist for **La source**
and **Coppélia.** He also was the librettist for Delibes' unperformed operatic work **La fille du golfe** (published 1859),
and the lyricist for two of Delibes' choruses.

Offenbach, Jacques (1819-1880): noted French composer,
primarily of operettas, who collaborated with Delibes on **Les
musiciens de l'orchestre,** an 1861 operatic work, and at
whose theater (Bouffes-Parisiens) nine of Delibes' early
operatic works were produced. Delibes posthumously completed two of Offenbach's works (**Belle Lurette,** 1880, and
Mamzelle Moucheron, 1881). Delibes was sufficiently close
to Offenbach to play practical jokes on him.

Orion (or Orione): a character in **Sylvia.** He is the dark
hunter who, rejected by Sylvia, abducts her to his cave from
which she later escapes. In the end the goddess Diana kills
Orion with her bow when he forces his way into the Temple of
Diana in an attempt to recapture Sylvia.

Reinach, Jacques, Baron de (1840-1892): collaborator with
Jules Barbier on the scenario for **Sylvia.**

Saint-Léon, Arthur (1821-1870): French dancer and choreographer who was the co-scenarist with Charles Nuitter for
La source and **Coppélia** and who also did the choreography
for both ballets.

Sangalli, Rita (1850-1909): Italian dancer who created the
title role in **Sylvia.**

Swanilda: principal female character in **Coppélia.** She is
engaged to Franz, who is infatuated by Coppélia, a beautiful

life-like mechanical doll created by Doctor Coppelius.
Jealous of Coppélia, Swanilda enters the toyshop of Doctor
Coppelius and discovers that her rival is only a doll. When
the toymaker tries to magically bring Coppélia to life,
Swanilda pretends to be the doll, gradually developing
living qualities and then performing two dances. Finally
she ceases the deception, leaves with Franz, and the couple
later marry.

Sylvia: principal female character in the ballet of that
name. She is one of the nymphs of Diana. Initially she
rejects the shepherd Aminta but later after some mytho-
logical-style adventures she is united in love with him.

Tchaikovsky, Peter Il'ich (1840–1893): prominent Russian
composer who strongly admired Delibes' music and who
probably copied the style of Delibes' ballets in his own
ballets. The two composers only met once, in 1886, and had
no other known contact.

Zandt, Marie van (1858–1919): American soprano for whom the
title role of **Lakmé** was especially written by Delibes, and
who had a great success in the role.

NOTABLE PERFORMANCES OTHER THAN PREMIERES

1878: La source produced at the Vienna Court under the title
Naïla. The 1867 divertissement **Valse, ou, Pas de fleurs**
by Delibes was included in the production, and thus the variant name **Naïla Waltz** was attached to the divertissement.

October 4, 1883: Lakmé's American debut at the Grand Opera
House in Chicago.

November 8, 1884: first production of **Coppélia** in Great
Britain, at the Empire Theatre, London, in an abridged
version.

November 25, 1884: first production of **Coppélia** in Russia,
at the Bolshoi Theater in St. Petersburg.

June 6, 1885: Lakmé's British debut at the Gaiety Theatre
in London.

March 11, 1887: Coppélia's debut in America, at the Metropolitan Opera House in New York.

December 2, 1901: Sylvia first produced in Russia, at the
Maryinsky Theater in St. Petersburg. Sergei Diaghilev was
to be involved with this, but a power struggle caused
Diaghilev's forced resignation from his position at the
Maryinsky and led to the eventual development of his famous

Ballets Russes company.

May 14, 1906: first full-length production of **Coppélia** in Great Britain, at the Empire Theatre in London.

May 18, 1911: **Sylvia** first produced in Great Britain, at the Empire Theatre in London, in an abridged version.

May 13, 1931: 1,000th performance of **Lakmé** at the Opéra-Comique in Paris.

September 3, 1952: the first full-length production of **Sylvia** in Great Britain, at Covent Gardent in London. This version was by Frederick Ashton.

1970: centenary production of **Coppélia** by the Royal Ballet at Covent Garden in London.

INDEXES

(The numbers refer to the bibliography entries, and
the A or D preceding the numbers refers to
the Adam or Delibes bibliographies.)

TITLE INDEX

(The numbers refer to the bibliography entries,
and the A or D preceding the numbers refer to
the Adam or Delibes bibliographies)

                              SUBJECT INDEX

         (The numbers refer to the bibliography entries,
         and the A or D preceding the numbers refers to
           the Adams or Delibes bibliographies.)